MW01275081

Free Pilgrim 3

— P I L G R I M —

 FriesenPress

Suite 300 - 990 Fort St
Victoria, BC, V8V 3K2
Canada

www.friesenpress.com

Copyright © 2021 by Pilgrim
First Edition — 2021

Photography contributions by May Fung

All rights reserved.

No part of this publication may be reproduced in any form, or by any means, electronic or mechanical, including photocopying, recording, or any information browsing, storage, or retrieval system, without permission in writing from FriesenPress.

ISBN
978-1-03-911180-6 (Hardcover)
978-1-03-911179-0 (Paperback)
978-1-03-911181-3 (eBook)

1. Travel, Essays & Travelogues

Distributed to the trade by The Ingram Book Company

Table of Contents

For my loving wife May "bashert" and constant companion with whom I share the joy-

For my understanding children Selena and Nigel from their imperfect father

For all the kind souls who decide to walk with me despite our differences

Introduction

Free Pilgrim 3 is a sequel to my book Free Pilgrim and Free Pilgrim 2 on my journeys down physical, spiritual, and mystical paths. This third book contains narratives of trips back to my home country and nine other trips to different places on this planet, which include, e.g., Ethiopia, Poland, Slovakia, Romania, Bulgaria, North Macedonia, and Albania (part of Eastern Europe) and a cruise to Paradise Bay to have a close-up view of the mighty continent of Antarctica.

It is my hope that Free Pilgrim 3 will bring joy to the armchair tourists who might find this book as close as they can get without booking tickets and setting out on their own. I also hope this publication will continue to motivate readers who are blessed with the opportunity to travel and intend to make similar journeys.

The Land Below The Wind

Many who have been friends or acquaintances of mine for more than 25 years know nothing or little about The Land Below The Wind (Sabah) - where I was born and raised. Still less, have they heard of Agnes Keith, who had spent considerable time, during the Japanese Occupation, in this part of the world, in what was then known as North Borneo. She was an American journalist born in Illinois and an author best known for her three autobiographical accounts of a life spent before, during and after the Second World War.

Agnes wrote three books: Land Below The Wind, Three Came Home and White Man Returns. She was married to an Englishman, Henry G. Keith, known as "Harry Keith". Henry Keith was the Conservator of Forests and Director of Agriculture for the government of North Borneo under the Chartered Company. But this is not the story about Agnes Keith. This is also not an autobiography of life spent in the land below the wind. North Borneo, as the names suggest, is situated on the northern portion of Borneo, the third-largest island in the world. It sits, below the Typhoon belt, bordering with the state of Sarawak to the southwest and the Kalimantan region of Indonesia to the south. It is watched over by the highest mountain in South East Asia, Mount Kinabalu, a world heritage site, with many plants that don't grow naturally anywhere else, including over eight hundred species of orchids. Endemism, of which the orchids are the best-known example with over 800 species.

For many westerners, the word Borneo conjures up images of White explorers with "Jungle Jim" hats and machetes in hand, slashing their way through the wild jungle teeming with ferocious animals, exotic plants, and roaming head-hunters.

The Land Below The Wind was kind to me. Someone once kindly mentioned to me that at the time of my appointment at the age of 33, I was the youngest Attorney-General ever appointed. I was also told that I had the lowest golf handicap for a sitting executive chairman of a bank and simultaneously as a President of a Golf and Country club. I count my blessings. I was baptised and raised in the Christian faith with Protestant Persuasion.

In this modern age and time, I am aware of Rudolf Bultmann's famous quote: "It is impossible to use electrical light and the wireless and to avail ourselves of modern medical and surgical discoveries, and the same time to believe in the New Testament world of spirits and miracles ...to do so is to make the Christian faith unintelligible and unacceptable to the modern world" ...To me, Science and Christianity complement each other. There is no reason for a Christian to fear good science. There is no need to fear Truth. Understanding the way God constructed our universe helps us human appreciate the wonder of creation. Our knowledge enables us to combat disease, ignorance, misunderstanding and bigotry. However, danger comes when we have a mindset to hold our faith in human knowledge (including scientific theories and suppositions) above the faith in our Creator.

WHERE IS HOME?

Returning to The Land Below The Wind will always be (for me) a journey down memory lane. I have always enjoyed going down memory lane, even though I know things do change with the passage of time. Several months ago, I met a fellow passenger on a Panama Canal cruise from Fort Lauderdale to San Diego. She was a former Malaysian of Chinese heritage, and her husband a Caucasian from the State of Washington. For some reason, they came and joined May and me at the Lido Restaurant on the Holland America Oosterdam. As was customary for me in trying to get to know someone, I asked her, "Where is home?" With that opener, the ice was broken, and thereafter we were engaged in conversation for quite a while. She was a retired registered nurse trained in England, but for her entire life, she had worked in a hospital in Seattle, Washington. As I had just drafted my article "Journey Back In Time", I brought up the subject of going down memory lane in England, a country where she had spent some time in her younger days.

In her version, she mentioned that she went back to England several years ago for her class reunion and was deeply disappointed because things had changed so much. She told me that she wished she had not gone there and had kept the memory of her good old days. I understood her and believed that her home is now in Seattle, where her heart is.

At the time of authoring this article, TripAdvisor informed me that I had travelled 1,633,351 miles and been to 74 countries but have only covered 56% of the world. I do not know nor understand how TripAdvisor did the calculation. However, I do realize, through all these wanderings and globetrotting as a pilgrim (www.freepilgrim. com), that there really is no ideal place on earth on which to live, and yet anywhere is ideal if it is "home." But I am just a descendant of the wandering Chinese Hakkas! So, where is "home" for me?

On the day before the rainy Canadian Astronomical Spring (before the Sun crossed the celestial equator on March 20th, 2018), I took a long transpacific flight "home" to Sabah to revisit the place in which I had spent more than half of my earthly life. Where I had, on countless occasions, heard the waves lapping lapping on the golden sand and on which I have traversed thousands of miles on her golf courses.

Even though I had travelled to Sabah for umpteen times, I still arrived "where I had started and known the place for the first time!" I disembarked at the Kota Kinabalu airport in this month of March 2018 with a mixing of memories and desire - stirring my root in the hot tropical sun with the intense craving for the famous seafood of Sabah and the delicious delicacies such as the famous Ice Kajang (ABC) at the Sabah Golf and Country and the Pisang Goreng (battered bananas deep-fried. Some are presented with cheese or chocolate or jam). I am given to understand that most people who migrate overseas from Sabah harbour the same desire for the taste of her varied cuisines.

Sabah and the rest of Borneo island were connected to mainland Asia about 20,000 years ago in a landmass known as the Sundaland. Subsequent climate change and deglaciation, which caused the global sea level to rise, resulted in the Sundaland being submerged, separating Borneo from the rest of Asia.

Stone tools and artefacts found in the Madai caves and in the archaeological site in Lake Tingkayu near the district of Kunak in Sabah have been estimated to date back from 28,000–17,000 years ago. The tools found there were considered advanced for its period. Head-hunters roamed within the borders of the island of Borneo in years past. The term can still strike fear among many in the western world.

Centuries ago, head-hunting by the Bornean indigenous natives was very much a part of life in this savage world on this remote island in the darkest heart of exotic Asia. These are not legends or native folklore. The ancestors of every North Bornean native tribes were head-hunters. Pictures taken of such human skulls showed that these things were very real. I went to the Monsopiad Cultural Village Penampang, near to Kota Kinabalu (the Capital of Sabah) and saw a collection of human skulls.

It is believed that these skulls form part of the collection of a well-known warrior and head-hunter by the name of Monsopiad. Some of the information provided may require collaboration. However, the elders who may have some knowledge about Monsopiad had already passed on. Head-hunting stopped soon after the British and missionaries arrived. Today the Monsopiad Cultural Village is a popular tourist's destination. During my recent visit, I witnessed the proud heritage of the natives in Sabah on grand display for tourists and visitors alike. Perhaps the natives have never felt (and I certainly have not heard about) victimisation by the British or the Christian missionaries. Maybe there were abuses by some, but the good of so many have not been buried with their bones as they have in North America.

On the Contrary, In the West (particularly in North America), we hear nothing but about "victimizations." Whether it is all about colour, race, creed, sex, or sexuality. However, Clarence Thomas, the second African American Supreme Court judge, said during an on-stage interview at the Library of Congress in Washington: "At some point, we're going to be fatigued with everybody being the victim". And he went on to say: "My grandfather would not let us wallow in that." Thomas added that he considers his grandfather "my hero and the single greatest human being I've ever met... With nine months of education. But he never saw himself as a victim." Clarence Thomas, born in 1948, was raised in Georgia coastal lowlands and spent his childhood working on his grandfather's farm. I wonder how many of us can relate to what he said. Roman Catholicism and Anglicanism arrived in North Borneo around the time of The North Borneo Chartered Company (also known as the British North Borneo Company) formed on 1 November 1881 to administer and exploit the resources of North Borneo. The Mill Hill missionary movement of the Roman Catholic Church focused mainly on indigenous communities, such as the Kadazan-Dusun people

Migration was also a key factor in the spread of Christianity. The Basel Mission also worked in North Borneo in 1882 among the migrant Hakka Chinese, many of whom were Christians who escaped after the Taiping Civil War. From that time on missionary, works have been carried out mainly by the majority denominations of Catholic, Anglican, Basel Christian Church of Malaysia (BCCM), Sidang Sijil Borneo (SIB) and Seventh Day Adventist (SDA). Today there are no less than 30 "denominations, independent churches or missions" in Sabah. Active ongoing church activities strengthened by missionary works and pastoral cares are the reason many of these independent churches are so attractive to both young and old alike.

I was born in North Borneo during the Second World War, grounded, raised, and received early education at Sung Siew (a Basel Mission School) in Sandakan. Life was hard during the War. We practically survived on cassava - better known to the West as tapioca which (according to Time Magazine publication) is one of the ten most dangerous food. The crop, if prepared incorrectly, can have deadly consequences.

Our family had taken an awfully long journey from the Middle Kingdom before ending up in Sandakan with Basel Mission which they were very actively involved. My great paternal grandfather had earlier left China at the end of the Taiping Civil War together with a group of indentured labourers for British Guyana to work in sugar cane plantations. Slavery had already ended by then. My paternal grandfather was later born. After a few years, they made their way back to China and eventually settled in Borneo (where my father and I were born) and I, blessed with the opportunity for education, went on to become a Barrister-at-law ... But that is another story http://www.freepilgrim.com/journey-back-in-time

Life is all about perceptions, how we see things. What has always fascinated me is that in America and to some extent in Canada, it is always a mistake for me to mention that I was by profession a "lawyer." I use the generic term "lawyer" as many in America do not know the difference between an English Barrister-at-law and an American attorney. My conversations with someone at a social gathering would end abruptly if I mentioned the profession. A priest once told me that he had the same experience and reaction if he mentioned that he is a priest. I do not understand why. On another occasion, I was having a wonderful conversation with a very charming lady at High Tea on a Royal Caribbean transatlantic cruise, but my conversation with her ended abruptly when I told her (with my poorly faked English accent) that I was born in Borneo...I also wondered why...Be that as it may... My journey continues from "The Land Below The Wind" to "The Land of The Rising Sun" ...

Note:

Research and discussions have revealed the major roles played by Christian missionaries in the progress of education in Sabah: Ref: CHRISTIANIZATION IN SABAH AND THE DEVELOPMENT OF INDIGENOUS COMMUNITIES: A HISTORICAL STUDY by MAT ZIN BIN MAT KIB *Journal of the Malaysian Branch of the* Royal Asiatic Society Vol. 77, No. 1 (286) (2004), pp. 53-65. Six Chief ministers of Sabah have studied at mission schools—The late Haji Mustapha (St. James Kudat), The late Donald Stephens (Sacred Heart), Joseph Parin and Peter Lo (St. Mary), Bernard Dompok (La Salle), Chong Ka Kiat and Musa Aman (All Saints)

The Land of The Rising Sun

Despite my travelling and globetrotting, I have not found many places on earth which blend ancient tradition and technical modernity quite like Japan - The Land of The Rising Sun. Centuries-old gardens and cobblestone walkways mingle in perfect harmony with modern soaring skyscrapers and dazzling neon signs. I first visited Japan during the Expo 1970 and have been back many times, not just to visit Honshu but also to spend some time in Kyushu, during my term as an Exco member of Malaysia-Japan Economic Association (MAJECA). Rudyard Kipling said: "The first condition of understanding a foreign country is to smell it." As a traveller (and I do not mean as a tourist) I had already smelled Japan but far from understanding the country. For many years I had taken the Japanese dish Tempura but never knew (until today informed by someone close to our family) that Tempura (the technique of dipping vegetables and sea food into a batter and frying them) was introduced by the Portuguese missionaries residing in Nagasaki in the 16th century!

I have since found out that the name "tempura" comes from the word "tempora" (meaning "times" or "time period" used by the Portuguese Catholic missionaries to refer to the Lenten period, Fridays, and other Christian holy days. "Quatuor tempora" refer to holy days when Catholics avoid meat and instead eat fish or vegetables. Hence, the etymology of the word "tempura ". The recipes for the dish today basically originated from the "Edo style", which was invented at the food stalls along the riverside fish market during the Edo period.

People relate Japan with Cherry Blossoms. Most tourists harbour the misunderstanding that cheery blossom season is in Spring. Actually, cheery blossoms open as early as January on the southern, subtropical islands of Okinawa. In contrast, on the northern island of Hokkaido, the flowering can be as late as in May. I arrived in Tokyo on April 18th but saw very few blooms even though the cheery blossom season there (as in Kyoto and Osaka) typically takes place in early April. Though late for cherry blossoms, we had the opportunity to immerse ourselves in exotic dining scenes and endless cultural encounters in the ever-evolving city of Tokyo and other beautiful parts of this fascinating country that were popular with international tourists such as Kyoto Kamakura and hakone.

Upon our arrival in Japan, someone close to us decided to show us Motomachi. With Yamate to the east and Kannai and Yamashitacho to the west, Motomachi became frequented by many foreigners soon after the start of the Meiji era.

The Minato-no-mieru-oka Park which we visited in Yamate, was a foreign settlement at the time of the opening of the port in Yokohama. What sets the Yamate district apart from other neighbourhoods in Yokohama is the gardens and western-style constructed houses. Yamate often referred to in English as The Bluff, is the name of a historic residential neighbourhood in Yokohama. The residential area was settled by western foreigners following the opening of Yokohama as a Treaty Port at the end of the Edo Period. The spreading scenery of the harbour and Yokohama Bay Bridge can be viewed from the observation deck at the park.

British House Yokohama is a designated cultural property of Yokohama originally built in 1937 as the British consular residence. It now part of the Rose Garden of Minato-no-mieru-oka Park. I learned that the roses here bloom from April to June and again from October to November. Many foreigners were buried in the Yokohama Foreign General Cemetery within the park. At the Gate House I saw a map on how to visit their graves. Photos of fascinating events associated with Yokohama (during the time as a Treaty Port) were displayed at the time of our visit. As we walked down the undulating roads and rolling hills, we saw a happy couple taking their photos.

On this day, we continued our stroll to the vibrant Yokohama China Town (founded by Chinese traders in 1859), where we saw friends indulging themselves in delightful activities. We also witnessed a Chinese lady making Xiaolongbao.

A Japanese friend once told me that Tokyo never sleeps. He must be referring to Kabukicho in Shinjuku. I visited Shinjuku in the late eighties and noticed that no other place in Tokyo seemed to be able to match its perpetual wakefulness. I decided to show my wife. We decided to have sashimi and yakisoba in one of the quaint restaurants and met a family from Portugal sitting next table to us. We struck up a conversation with the daughter Katherine who now works in Berlin. She told us that Members of the world-famous Berlin Philharmonic Orchestra regularly perform on Tuesdays free of charge at lunchtime in the striking foyer of the Philharmonic concert hall...We have made a note of that information!

Travelling by ourselves in Honshu (with the help of the Japan Rail Pass), my wife and I found the opportunity to immerse ourselves in the culture of this fascinating country. I also had a plan for us to visit some port cities in Northern Japan. I ordered two weekly Passes from JBT International (Canada) Ltd and collected them myself at their office at 900 Georgia St. Vancouver instead of having them mailed to us. The Passes are tokens vouchers that we redeemed for weekly Pass tickets at the JR East ticket office (which had a long queue) upon our arrival at Narita International Airport.

Trains symbolise modernity in Japan. Shinkansen (bullet train) cut journeys between Tokyo and Osaka by two hours when it opened in 1964. If one has a Japan Rail Pass, this route can be very economical. However, two of the fastest shinkansen trains, the Nozomi on the Tokaido Line and the Mizuho on the Sanyo line, are not covered by the Japan Rail Pass. Today we took the Shinkansen Hikari bullet train from Shinagawa Station to Kyoto, passing Nagoya in less than 3 hours.

KYOTO-

A visit to Japan is not complete without visiting Kyoto. Nijo-jo Castle in Kyoto has witnessed some of the most dramatic and notable events in Japanese history since it was constructed in 1603. It is now a UNESCO World Heritage Site, and Kyoto City began full-scale restoration of the Castle in 2011. The 400 -year-old building of the Ninomaru-Goten Palace and the Kara mon Gate are unique survivals of the early Edo period ornate Japanese architecture and de sign.

KAMAKURA -

Kamakura, as a coastal city with a high number of seasonal festivals as well as its ancient Buddhist and Shinto shrines and temples, is a popular domestic tourist destination in Japan

HAKONE –

Hakone is situated in a mountainous region mountain peak (3,776.24 m) in Japan. Aside from its fabulous views of that iconic volcano and Lake Ashi, Hakone is spectacular on its own. With quick and convenient rail and bus connections, it can easily be visited as a day trip from Tokyo. We got to Hakone (with the JR Pass) by taking the longer but scenic train route on the slower Tokaido Line via Olfuna to Odawara to connect with Hakone Tozan railway and return with the Tokaido Shinkansen to Shinagawa. The beauty of Kanagawa can be seen by a slow train from Shinagawa to Odawara on JR Tokaido Line.

Photographing at popular destinations can be challenging when hundreds of tourists visit the same sites as we do and at the same exact time. Many people, oblivious to us, appeared in my camera frame. Tourists yelled, interfering with the serenity of the place. It is understandable that sometimes we want the place all to ourselves.

But sometimes people come into our lives for a good reason. Complete strangers help us along the way. On one occasion, after visiting the Resurrection Cathedral in Tokyo, we decided to see the Senso-Ji Shrine, an ancient Buddhist temple located in Asakusa Tokyo and one most significant. After walking for quite a distance, we realized that we were probably in the wrong direction. Then a stranger appeared and came into our lives, walk with us and showed us how to get to the location of the Shrine!...

While the Shinkansen can be quiet and comfortable riding, the commuter ta rain is a different story. There is nothing quite like riding in commuter trains during the rush hour in Tokyo. We found out and experienced it on the way back to our hotel in Tsurumi from Akihabara, where we had spent the morning and early afternoon. The rush-hour ride taught us deferential Canadians how to assert ourselves in a jampacked train ☺. Having spent time in a megacity like London in my younger days, I was much more comfortable (than my wife) standing cheek by jowl with people on subway trains crammed shoulder to shoulder.

On this journey, I decided not only to revisit the many crowded iconic sites in Honshu popular with tourists but also to visit other equally (for me) significant sites less visited by international tourists. As a pilgrim, I am naturally interested in seeing some churches whenever I visit a new place and find myself as a stranger in town.

Christianity was introduced to Japan during the Edo- era (1603–1868) by Jesuits missionaries from Portugal. Christian missionaries, such as Francis Xavier, were among the first to travel to Japan to teach Catholicism. However, somehow the influence of the West and the religious aspect eventually came into conflict with the Tokugawa shogunate. The Sakoku Edict was issued in 1635. Christianity was banned under the Edict. The daimyō and samurai persecuted missionaries and believers. For more than two centuries, Christian's devotees went into hidings on some remote islands to continue practising their faith. The ban on Christianity was lifted in the early Meiji period (1868–1912). Many churches were built, most in the South West of Japan. Oura Cathedral (the oldest standing church in Japan) was constructed in Nagasaki City after the end of Japan's era of seclusion when freedom of religion was granted. It served a growing community of foreign merchants who took up residence in Nagasaki. A number of these sites are expected to receive World Heritage status.

I was also blessed with the opportunity to pay a visit to The Neo-Byzantine Cathedral (commonly known as Nikolai-do) situated in Chiyoda Tokyo. The founder of the Cathedral, Ivan Dmitrievich Kasatkin (1836-1912), later St. Nicholas (Kasatkin), spent his first seven years in Japan studying the Japanese language culture and religion. He was 25 when he first came to Japan as a young priest assigned to the Russian consulate in Hakodate. St. Nicholas introduced Orthodox Christianity to the local community and translated the scriptures and many liturgical books and prayer books into Japanese, all of which are still in use today.

The Yokohama Kaigan Kyokai (church) situated Naka-Ku Yokohama was founded in 1872 as the first Protestant Church in this country. The founder and first pastor, Rev. J. H. Ballagh, encountered considerable difficulties in his initial missionary activities. Japanese who developed personal contacts with Christian's missionaries in Yokohama started to gather on this site, and Rev. Ballagh stood up and read Isaiah 32:15 "until the Spirit is poured upon us from high and the wilderness becomes a fruitful field, and the fruitful field is deemed a forest." But according to the World Values Survey, Japan remains one of the most secular nations in the world. There may be up to 3 million Japanese Christians in Japan (US State Department 2007 Religious Freedom Report retrieved on 2011-06-15.) spread among many denominational affiliations.

AOMORI -

We made a brief call at the port of Aomori and were greeted by a site for the prefecture's highest educational facility. Group of enthusiastic students. Aomori is the only prefectural capital in Japan that has no national university.

Nearby Hirosaki became the site for the prefecture's highest educational facility. We met a person from Philadelphia who wanted so much to see a bit of Aomori, but she had great difficulty doing because of her physical condition.

Hakodate is in the centre of the Kameda Peninsula of Hokkaido, famous for its seafood market (though less known as Tsukiji fish market in Tokyo). A short walk from Hakodate Station can be found the bustling Hakodate Asaichi (Morning Market), tempting visitors with an array of delectable fresh Hakodate produce

Hakodate was one of few contact points of Japan with the outside world. It became host to several overseas consulates. During that time, the Russian consulate included a chapel from where Nicholas of Japan is credited with introducing Eastern Orthodox Christianity to Japan in 1861 (now the Japanese Orthodox Church). The historical missionary churches are neighbouring churches, including the Roman Catholic and the Anglican Church...

MURORAN - AND WE PROCEEDED TO MURORAN...

Despite some and occasional cruise ships calling at this port (as if by accident), Muroran is definitely not a vacation destination. Most cruise ships would berth for a brief time and then sail off with their demanding passengers to less grimy destinations. Along the coast by the port is such unalloyed ugliness that it brings tears to those aesthetically sensitive. Concrete is to be sure, a wonderful thing, but do ugly concrete structures have to be situated along the shore? Why is progress so antagonistic to purity and beauty? This is a very pertinent question indeed!

However, Cape Chikyu, not far from the port of Muroran, is not without its share of rugged mighty cliffs! Beauty endowed by mother nature. Few tourists go to Cape Chikyu. We were game to trek up the steep hill on the country road, but as we ascended, the vegetation, get less and less luxuriant, which proved how difficult it was the struggle for trees to exist (except for the humble grass) on this stony hill. At the very top of the hill, we were rewarded with the opportunity to shoot photos of the spectacular ocean view below with a small lighthouse as a backdrop. Much has been written in nature books, love stories and poems about the beauty and loveliness of flowers, but I find it very strange indeed that we should overlook the simple beauty and usefulness of the humble wild grass adorning and supporting the bare earth and mighty cliff!

At the very top, there is a Bell of Happiness. It was suggested to us by a local to give it a ring, and we both did ☺...and my Journey continues...

Just a thought: Life is all about how we see things. As a Christian, the right perspective is shown to us only by the Holy Spirit when we allow it to dwell within us...

Journey Along The Walls

"As I strolled along these mighty walls
Securing my steps for fear of a fall
I imagined that I have seen what came before
and realized that I just simply watched them in awe
But never really understood the necessity of them all!"

– Nicholas Fung

It knocked me over with a feather to hear conservatives used the word "progressive" to describe the liberals or the left, giving the word a bad connotation. Man has the incredible ability to invent things that were unforeseeable 50, maybe even 20 years ago. There is much progress, and we continue to advance. I am no longer a child of the rotary dial phone era. The digital age (with the proliferation of mobile devices and other technology) is catapulting the world to a new dimension with effective communications and methods of expression. Social media has played a significant role in politics and religious institutions. I am aware that progress has given me this digital phone in my breast pocket for communications and photographs. I hope to make effective use of this technical modernity. Perhaps utilize this smart camera phone to capture and immortalise some "moments" or captivating scenes for sharing with the many generations of children yet unborn. But I realize that shooting photographs of people, not objects, with this camera phone is a different matter. If I take a photo of a primitive person with this camera phone and show it to him, he would probably think it is a miracle. Whereas if I take the photograph of superstitious modern humans, he may be offended because he thinks a photo of him has taken away a part of his soul!

Much has been written in poems and love stories about the beauty of nature, but little attention is drawn or credit accorded to the gifted and grand construction by Man. These constructions, once destroyed, are lost forever! What could be grander than the old churches, castles, and ancient walls? This is a journey along the walls. "Wall" comes from the Latin word "vallum." Another Latin word, "murus", means a defensive stone wall ... My perspective and perception of walls are pretty limited because we are now living in an open society. I could not really understand why walls were constructed throughout human history. Perhaps strolling along some of the famous walls around the world may shed some light for me on this matter.As I understand, states have been building walls since ancient times. Some were quite effective, others less so. People have been kept in with walls built by Authoritarian Regimes. Is the construction of walls morally wrong? At the core also lies a fundamental question: What can walls realistically accomplish?

Dubrovnik, Croatia, with its magnificent walled city, remains one of my favourite cities in the world. With its superb location, overlooking the calm blue waters of the Adriatic, it is undoubtedly one of the world's most magnificent walled cities. It was once the capital of the wealthy sea-faring Republic of Ragusa (1358-1808), and today it is a UNESCO heritage site.

In the 16th century, at the peak of its golden age, it had one of the largest merchant fleets in the world, and the people became extremely rich. The residents were living sophisticated lifestyles, and they valued refinements and the arts. I was blessed with two enlightened visits to the limestone-paved streets of the city's Old Town. I discovered the city's churches, monasteries and palaces and walked the 1.2 miles (2 km) of walls first built in the 12th century.

Croatia is just a stone throw away from the country of Montenegro. In fact, they share a common border, yet until today, I had never set foot on this little-known Balkan state, which is now a new member of NATO. Hence, I decided to make a trip; to get a glimpse into the history and culture of Montenegro and walk the walled city of Kotor. This southeastern European country is the newest member of NATO since the Alliance's first expansion in 2009 when Croatia joined. The accession of Montenegro to the alliance of NATO took place on 5 June 2017. The arrival of Montenegro as the latest member of NATO appears to be a sign of the Alliance's continuing relevance at a time of renewed tensions in Europe. To spread a security blanket across Europe's once fractious south-eastern flank (after the bitterly fought Balkan wars), NATO is thinking of bringing the new democracies of the region into its fold.

MONTENEGRO

On this journey, putting geopolitics aside, I found myself in a situation to be dazzled at a distance by the shimmering Adriatic Sea and enjoyed the beautiful Bay of Kotor dotted with medieval villages flanked by towering craggy mountains.

We visited the UNESCO World Heritage site of Kotor. This old town of Kotor has all the features of a typical Mediterranean town: antique monuments, small shops, narrow streets, and picturesque buildings. This is where its history, culture, and tradition are being preserved. The town was settled during Ancient Roman times when it was known as Acruvium. It was first mentioned in 168 BC. It has been fortified since the early Middle Age, became part of the Venetian Republic in 1420, and except for two short periods of Ottoman rule, it remained under Venice until 1797. It served as a naval base during the first World War. The fortifications of Kotor are an integrated historical fortification system (that protected the medieval town of Kotor) containing ramparts, bastions, gates, a castle, and ancillary concrete structures. Together with the old city and its natural surroundings, the fortifications were inscribed in the list of World Heritage Sites in 1979. These were military architectures of the past, of Illyria, Byzantium, Italian and Austrian. We approached the castle through the picturesque gate from which we had the perfect view... the ideal view of the old city! I endeavoured (without success) to picture this place as it was in its supreme glory. It was a perfect day for us to see the hoary castle and its wall with the feeling I was on hallowed and haunted ground.

"To muse, to creep, to halt at will, to gaze" – William Wordsworth

I have visited many similar fortified villages with walls around the European trail through my globetrotting and have always harboured mixed feelings about these ancient, fortified cities. From the perspective of early civil engineering, it has always appeared to me that the construction is imposing, and the walls of Kotor are no exception. It is a living monument to the story of Kotor. The wall appears to me to be frozen in time within the contrast of the streets, the new buildings, and the larger city's modern technology. To me, walls recount an important aspect of the historical narrative of Kotor and those of many walled cities worldwide. As the contemporary visitor viewing it from the present perspective, I harbour a feeling of incongruity about the aesthetic design and planning of a town being encased in such a solid and forbidding mass. Perhaps I should understand that the incumbents at the material time might have had less desire to quibble over architectural niceties when their priority really was more inclined towards safety and security. Yes, safety and security! The importance of fending off belligerent attackers and invaders would undoubtedly take precedence over artistic necessity.

CHINA

As we strolled along in Kotor, I could not help thinking about the Great Wall of China, an ancient series of walls and fortifications, totalling more than 13,000 miles in length conceived by Emperor Qin Shi Huang. Emperor Qin Shi Huang had proclaimed himself the first emperor of China in 221 B.C. and laid an extraordinary underground treasure of an entire army of life-size terra cotta soldiers and horses which have been interred for more than 2,000 years) as a means of preventing incursions from barbarian nomads!

VATICAN CITY

I also recall visiting the wall surrounding present-day Vatican City. History shows that back in 846, the Saracens raiders looted St. Peter's Basilica and the Papal Basilica of St. Paul outside the walls. In consequence thereof, Pope Leo IV created the Leonine Wall surrounding Vatican Hill. Additional defences were added in the 15th and 16th centuries.

JERUSALEM

Except for brief intermittent periods, the city of Jerusalem has been surrounded by walls since ancient times. In the period known in biblical terms as the era of the Patriarchs, a town named Jebus was built and well-fortified on the southern hill of Jerusalem. When Rome destroyed the Second Temple in 70 A.D, only one outer wall remained standing - known as the "Western Wall". The Western Wall "Hakotel Hama'aravi" is all that remains of the Jerusalem temple where Jesus taught and prayed. This wall formed part of the plaza upon which stood the remodelled temple of Herod the Great. It is an ancient limestone wall in the Old City of Jerusalem. The total height of the Wall from its foundation is estimated at 105 feet (32 m), with the exposed section standing approximately 62 feet (19 m) high.

The Wall consists of 45 stone courses, 28 above ground and 17 underground. The first seven visible layers are from the Herodian period. This section of wall is built from an enormous Meleke limestone block, possibly quarried at Zedekiah's Cave. During the reign of the Ottoman Empire,

Sultan Suleiman the Magnificent decided to fully rebuild the Jerusalem city walls, partly on the remains of the ancient walls. Being built between and 1541, they are currently the walls that exist and surround the city of Jerusalem. It is significant to note that at the time of my visit to the walled city of Kotor, the United States was politically embroiled on the topic of building a wall in her Southern border. Attorney General Jeff Sessions (referencing the Bible) said God told Nehemiah to build a wall when he got back to Jerusalem. "That's the first thing he told him to do," Sessions said. "It wasn't to keep people in. It was to keep bad people out. I don't think there is a scriptural basis that justifies any idea that we must have open borders in the world today."

It is essential to observe that there were many episodes of opposition to Nehemiah's mission. The resistance gradually intensified. Opposition came from Sanballat and Tobiah (Nehemiah 2:10) to the addition of Geshem, the Samarians, the Arabs, Ammonites, and Ashdodites (Nehemiah 4:7. The opposition climaxed to "all our enemies" (Nehemiah 6:16). The adversaries were hostile, moving from displeasure (Nehemiah 2:10) through "mockery" and "ridicule" to threats of physical violence (Nehemiah 4:8) and malicious personal attacks (Nehemiah 6:1-9). Despite this opposition, Nehemiah worked tirelessly at his appointed task. He finished building the walls of Jerusalem in a remarkable fifty-two days (Nehemiah 15:1).

During the Second Intifada that began in September 2000, Israel constructed The Israeli Wall as a security measure against terrorism. The Israeli government defended its construction as necessary to stop the wave of violence inside Israel that the uprising had brought with it. The wall (initially presented as a temporary security measure in a time of heightened tensions) has since been rapidly associated with a future political border between Israel and Palestine. In the July 9, 2004, advisory opinion, the International Court of Justice advised that the barrier is a violation of international law.

The Israeli government says that the barrier has been effective as the number of suicide bombings carried out from the West Bank fell during the relevant periods from 73 to 12. On February 20, 2004, the World Council of Churches (while acknowledging the grave security concerns of Israel asserted that the construction of the barrier on its own territory would not have been a violation of international law) called on member Churches, Ecumenical Councils of Churches, Christian World Communions, and specialized ministries of churches to condemn the wall as an act of unlawful annexation.

The contentious issue of the wall continues unresolved. Pope Francis, on another occasion, reiterated that we should be building bridges instead of walls! Currently, the partial federal government shutdown in the United States enters its fourth week without a deal to re-open the government, as both sides dig in over the funding for building the Southern wall bordering with Mexico. The semantic appear to e changing the time I write this article, but "Steel slats, concrete barriers, or bollard-style fences – they are all the same." History will record whether the Southern wall of the United States would ever be built.

BERLIN

The construction of the Berlin Wall started in 1961. It separated the country of Germany for a whole generation. On 12 June 1987, President Ronald Reagan, at the Brandenburg Gate, challenged General Secretary Mikhail Gorbachev to tear down the Wall as a symbol of increasing freedom in the Eastern Bloc. President Reagan said, "We welcome change and openness; for we believe that freedom and security go together, that the advance of human liberty can only strengthen the cause of world peace. There is one sign the Soviets can make that would be unmistakable, that would advance dramatically the cause of freedom and peace. General Secretary Gorbachev, if you seek peace, if you seek prosperity for the Soviet Union and eastern Europe, if you seek liberalization, come here to this gate. Mr Gorbachev, open this gate."

"Mr Gorbachev, tear down this wall." The fall of the Berlin Wall began on the evening of 9 November while I was in Hamburg for the World Economic Forum1989. Hamburg for the World Economic Forum1989.

I have been groping blindly for insight into the necessity of walls in our lives. I had an enlightening conversation with a structural engineer friend of mine who is no fan of President Donald Trump. I asked him why we needed walls for our houses. He told me that they were to hold up the roofs! Then I asked him why the doors were there. He said the doors were only for decoration purpose! A Jewish friend once told me that the Western (Wailing) Wall is no mere historical asset. It is the Jewish root. At the Western Wall, the Jews watered the Wall with their tears and melted the stones with their kisses. I am informed that Jerusalem was destroyed and rebuilt nine times. And through it all, one symbol remained intact:

The Western Wall

In establishing the eternal covenant with Abraham, God promised that the Jewish people would never be destroyed (Genesis 17:7). The Western (Wailing) Wall thus became the symbol of both devastations and of hope. The Wall is a symbol of the Jewish people. There have been many efforts to destroy the Wall, and yet it remains eternal. Will the Jewish people outlive their enemies and remain eternal? As Mark Twain wrote: "...Other peoples have sprung up and held their torch high for a time, but it burned out, and they sit in twilight now or have vanished. The Jew saw them all, beat them all... All things are mortal but the Jew; all other forces pass, but he remains. What is the secret of his immortality?" God warned the people of Israel not to listen to false voices (Jeremiah 29:8-9). The same is true for all of us. All these false voices can be deafening. What is the way I can navigate the cacophony of opinions which come barreling at me? I believe that knowing our Creator and His voice, we can hear Him above the noise and feel in His guidance through the Holy Spirit.

Just a thought:

Do physical walls really matter? Some say walls are premedieval but so are wheels. Perhaps walls, it is arguable, may not be in every country's best interests. I realize perhaps there is somewhere we all can agree on the necessity of walls, i.e. the invisible walls: in cyberspace.

"Every wall is a door." – Ralph Waldo Emerson

"There are no constraints on the human mind. No walls around the human spirit. No barriers to our progress except those we ourselves erect"
– Ronald Reagan

Rise From The Ashes

As I started paying more attention, I have noticed on labels the word "ash" in measurements in grams listed (as a component) about the nutrient content of food. While we might picture the leftover residue at the bottom of the fireplace, ash is a general term that can refer to several substances in our food. I am informed that ash refers to any inorganic material, such as minerals, present in food and can include both compounds with essential minerals (such as potassium and calcium) and toxic materials (such as mercury). Everyone has a different perception of the meaning of "Rise From The Ashes." In the proper context or circumstance and without pomp, we would speak of a "come back." In popular culture, the allegorical symbol, the phoenix, which symbolises rebirth, often appear. In Greek mythology, a phoenix is a bird that cyclically regenerates itself or is otherwise born again. In another classical mythology, the phoenix, which lived for five hundred years in the Arabian desert, would burn itself on a funeral pyre ignited by the sun and then reborn itself from the ashes with renewed youth to live through another cycle of life.

The simile "like a phoenix from the ashes" is used to describe someone or something that has made a fresh start after experiencing destruction. For Christians, ash is used on Ash Wednesday. The ashes usually come from the burnt Palms of the previous year's Passion Sunday celebration. So, these ashes bring Christians back to the last celebration of the Passion, Death and Resurrection of Jesus. On the first day of Lent, Christians begin a journey of renewal - from death to life.

PRAGUE TO DRESDEN

We were in the Czech Republic during our "sojourn" in Central Europe in the month of October 2018. I had rented an Ab&b studio apartment at Soukenicka in Prague, where we intended to stay for a short while to with the hope of immersing ourselves in the culture of this beautiful old city. As Dresden in Eastern Germany is only approximately 150 km by road from our studio in Prague, I had (in the process of planning for this Central Europe sojourn) determined to pay the city a visit. We decided to take the Flixbus coach to Dresden. It took us about 15-20 mins walk from our studio to the UAN Florenc Station in Prague.

I had my backpack on and really "didn't feel old" even though I squirmed and felt uncomfortable at the thought of the cliché. I wouldn't say I liked the look as I caught a glimpse of myself in the reflection on the shop window or the parked car's side mirror. This was not the person who drove the Lotus Elan not so long ago. Then I remembered bus drivers having a second look at me when I showed them my senior's bus ticket. Age is indeed a matter of perspective.

The trip by Flixbus took us in less than two hours from Prague to Dresden. We checked into the Intercity Hotel in the new city square, which was only a short walk from the Dresden main train station. The counter staff at the hotel upgraded us to a larger (and quieter) room and gave us two free city transport tickets valid for two days even though the centre of the historic district is within a 10-15 mins walk away. This was the perfect location as it was also near a few trams stops, and we did make use of the tickets for numerous tram rides taking us over the river into a lively district called Neustadt, or the "New Town."

Lying on the scenic Elbe Riverbank, the city of Dresden is lush and filled with gardens and parks. It is one of the greenest cities in all of Europe, with 63% of the city being green areas and forests. It is rich in arts and culture. The great opera composer Wilhelm Wagner debuted a number of works here in the 1800s. The melange of styles reflected in the cityscapes would satisfy most people who are interested in museums and architecture.

As for me, the focus of my journey to this city was the newly rebuilt Frauenkirche. I was informed that 75% of the historical centre of Dresden was destroyed by Allied bombing in 1945. Dresden was the seventh-largest city of Germany and a cultural centre known as the "Florence on the Elbe." Dresden was a wonderfully beautiful baroque city and all that was best in Germany. However, it is said that it also contained all the worst from Germany during the Nazi period. But why Dresden? Some noted that from a military perspective, no one understands why the city was targeted. The end of the war was already in sight, and Dresden had no garrisons.

From another perspective, though a centre for the arts, Dresden was also one of Germany's most significant remaining industrial sites. It had over 100 factories of various sizes; some of these were facilities for producing artilleries, aircraft components and poison gas. In addition, it was a key hub with railway lines running north to Berlin and south to Prague and Vienna. Rails also ran to Munich, Leipzig, and Hamburg. It was the most significant remaining city in the Third Reich, not yet bombed by the Allied Forces. On the night of February 13, 1945, the RAF reduced Dresden's 18th-century cathedral to rubble in an air raid. The destruction of Dresden was epically tragic. The bombing by the British Royal Air Force has become a symbol of excessive violence on the part of the Allies Forces during World War II.

After the fall of the Berlin Wall, with the reunification of Germany and a period of reconstruction, Dresden once again returned to a position of prominence in German cultural life. The historical centre is nowadays largely restored to its former glory. However, some parts of the city are still under reconstruction. At the time of our visit in October 2018, Dresden boasts more than 50 art galleries, 40 museums and 30 theatres. This includes the "Green Vault," a unique museum boasting a collection of former royal treasures.

The reconstructed **Dresden Frauenkirche**, the focus of my visit to Dresden, is a Lutheran church with a statue of Martin Luther standing visibly for every visitor to behold. The much earlier old church building was Catholic until it became Protestant during the reformation. The old church was replaced in the 18th century by a larger Baroque Lutheran building. The original baroque church, designed by Dresden's city architect George Bähr (one of the greatest masters of German Baroque style), was constructed between 1726 and 1743. It was regarded as the finest baroque building north of the Alps. But in consequence of an air raid on February 13, 1945, the Cathedral collapsed. Nothing was done to it after the War under Communist Rule. For more than 45 years, the residents of Dresden viewed the Church as nothing but a mound of rubble flanked by two jagged walls.

In 1989, with the unification of Germany, a noted Dresden musician Ludwig Güttler headed a 14-member group of enthusiasts to form a Citizens' Initiative. Consequently, "The Society to Promote the Reconstruction of the Frauenkirche" emerged. An enthusiastic and aggressive private fund-raising campaign began. The organization grew to over 5,000 members in Germany and 20 other countries. The project gathered momentum as hundreds of architects, art historians, and engineers began sorting out the thousands of stones, identifying and labelling each for reuse in the new structure. Others worked to raise money. "The church is to Dresden what St Paul's is to London. This is true both architecturally and psychologically," said Dr Paul Oestreicher, a Canon emeritus of Coventry Cathedral and a founder of the Dresden Trust. The new Frauenkirche finished in 2005, is now considered one of the greatest pieces of architecture in the world.

The Frauenkirche is a centralised octagonal building, i.e. the lower part of the church has the form of an octagon. There are seven doors leading into the main church. The structure is topped by four corner towers and crowned by a circular dome built totally of sandstone with a stone "lantern." With its height of 24 m and diameter of 26 m, it is said to be the largest stone dome north of the Alps. The dome's shape is also unique and distinctive on many counts with the curved base giving it a bell-like look. This is why Trebuchet MS (Body) the Frauenkirche was also nicknamed the 'Stone Bell', which was finished in 2005 and is now considered one of the world's greatest pieces.

As we entered the church, we were completely mesmerised by the beauty of its interior. I was given to understand that large chunks of statues, like the one depicting Moses, were cleaned and incorporated into the new structure. Eighty per cent of the altar was reconstructed using the original materials. It seemed to me that the pulpit was nearer to the centre of Chancel, and it made me wonder whether this physical location of the pulpit is one of the visual affirmations of the rudiments of Lutheranism.

An opportunity has also been provided for everyone to visit the fantastic baroque interior and walk-up (within the dome) to the "lantern" to look at the reconstructed city below. For many years, the ruins and now the newly rebuilt Frauenkirche acts as a call for peace among the different nations of the world. I am given to understand that since its completion in 2005, the Frauenkirche foundation's emphasis for the church (besides preservation) has moved towards using it for charitable and religious purposes.

We ascended the cupola to the "lantern" and did enjoy, from all directions, the spectacular views of the city and the surrounding countryside. Further up the "lantern" on the top of the church sits the new tower cross in its rightful place. I am informed that a group of donors from Britain had paid for the cross, in a sort of British mea culpa for the bombing! The silversmith who built the new cross is the son of one of the British bomber pilots who participated in the massive firebombing raid on the night of February 13, 1945, which killed tens of thousands of people. Dresden Bishop Jochen Bohl said in a sermon during the consecration service: "A deep wound that has bled for so long can be healed. From hate and evil, a community of reconciliation can grow, which makes peace possible." The Church, reconsecrated on October 30, 2005, has demonstrated the possibility of rebirth and has risen from the ashes of the Second World War.

Perhaps the reconstruction of the Frauenkirche has made this church a symbol of peace and reconciliation.

Journey to Peace and Joy

I have just lit the third candle in the Season of Advent 2018, the season of hope, peace, joy, and love. I thought about Christmas. If we understand ourselves, we know the meaning of this season. From the time humans existed, every soul has deep longings. Some of us find purpose and know there is more to this life of earthly existence. Some of us may deny it, but it is nonetheless true for all of us. I am thankful and cannot discount the blessings, the episodes of awe, moments of happiness and exhilarations in my life.

In retrospect, there were moments in my life when I could really say, "That was wonderful." From the Library of Congress, I have just received a Certificate of Registration issued under the Copyright Office, which attests that registration for my book "Free Pilgrim 2" has been made a part of the Copyright Office records. That was also wonderful! I have always had the temptation to tell relatives and friends that the stories in my books are essential. I share my stories because I care and hope they read them.

Before leaving on this journey to Central Europe, I had read a research study conducted by UBC and McGill University that found Vancouver, where I reside, as the unhappiest city in Canada. Even though the London-based Economist Intelligence Unit (EIU) ranked it 6th among the ten most "livable" cities globally, Vancouver had fallen three spots from its third-place position in 2017's survey. Perhaps happiness is found not in how much we have obtained but in how little we demand? Maybe the cost of living is high, and we Vancouverites are being caged in some way? "The greatest need of our time is to clean out the enormous mass of mental and emotional rubbish that clutters our minds." – Thomas Merton. Perhaps we need to be freed of these clutters? But when we live on the edge in this confusing world, in this uncertain time of cacophony and war of deception, who will set us free?

On a cool Autumn day in October 2018, after two hours by Flixbus, we arrived at Karlovy Vary from the old city of Prague, Czech Republic. Upon arrival, we could not find a taxi stand at the Bus Terminus but were fortunate enough that an unoccupied taxi was passing by and the driver could speak some English. We piled our two suitcases into the limited space of the trunk of his small car. I could see he was eyeing us in the rear-view mirror. He probably found it strange that a Chinese couple would arrive at the world-famous Spa Town of Karlovy Vary (Carlsbad) by Flixbus. The road to our hotel was a bit winding. It appeared to me that our driver knew every corner and turn of the road. He was driving speedily doing the car. Nevertheless, we arrived at Hotel Petr safely.

We checked into the hotel but did not like it and felt uncomfortable with the room we were assigned. There was a funny feeling that we needed to change the room. Peace came to us the moment we settled down in the Charles suite. I had just successfully persuaded the lady at the check-in counter to reassign us to this room which overlooked the Colonnade. It was not really the so-called "gift of the gap" but rather my age that did most of the persuasion.

From time immemorial hot springs have arisen on the confluence of the rivers Ogre and Teplá, approximately 130 km (81 mi) west of Prague. Karlovy Vary is world-famous for Hydrotherapy. We did not take any spa treatment during our visit. We were advised that the therapeutic procedure entailed several phases, i.e. the Input (adaptation) phase (1st to 10th day), the custom treatment phase (2nd or 3rd week) and the Down phase (the end of the 3rd week or possibly the 4th week).

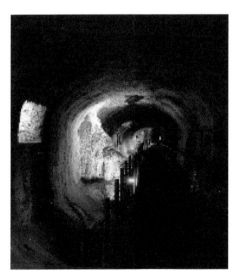

However, we did explore the underground thermal springs and tasted the Karlovy Vary thermal mineral water of various temperatures ranging from 55.6 degrees Celsius of the Trzni Kolonada to 72 degrees Celsius of the Vridelni Kolonada with spouted ceramic drinking cups which we purchased from the nearby stall. I am informed that the Karlovy Vary thermal mineral water compose of a highly concentrated mix of natural substances. Over 40 elements necessary for the human body are analysed. The Springs have similar composition but differ mainly in temperature and the quantity of carbon dioxide, other gases, and trace elements, thereby giving different tastes and healing effects. Even though the thermal hot spring water quality has not changed over the centuries, its usage has evolved. Today the Drinking Cure is a fundamental treatment procedure in Karlovy Vary. We were advised that the drinking cure positively affects the entire digestive tract and motor system. It stimulates insulin secretion in people with diabetes and reduces cholesterol, but it is not advisable to combine the therapeutic cure with the consumption of alcohol, tobacco, cannabis etc.

It is no secret that the air quality in Vancouver, where I reside (though better than that of most major cities), is not conducive to a healthy lifestyle. Besides, we are also aware of the negative effects a sedentary lifestyle has on the "disease" of civilization. Over dinner, we discussed and determined to make an early start the next morning to explore this lovely town on foot, as we always do when able. As a pilgrim, I try always to visit a church in an unfamiliar location. I had read that the Russian Orthodox Church of Saint Peter and Paul, Karlovy Vary, is the country's largest and most important orthodox church. We walked from our hotel to this church, passing the old Anglican Church of St. Luke, which had already been converted into a museum.

The golden domes of Saint Peter and Paul attracted our attention from a distance as they shone in the sun on this bright sunny day of our visit. The church was still under reconstruction during our visit, but we were allowed to enter it. It is a single-aisle church of Byzantine style. Although we could not see much of the interior, we were still able to enjoy its exquisite white, and blue exteriors with the murals of saints painted on them. The visit to this church became one of the highlights of our trip to this Spa Town.

We walked slowly down the road from the Church, noticing a group of elderly hikers playing like school children in the park opposite. A girl bunched her scarf up and sat on it in the middle of the field while watching her friends playing frisbee in the Autumn wind. I spent the next hour watching the sky and at the trees with leaves falling and twirling down toward me, coming into my line of vision, and then being whisked off to the side by the wind or a passing car. As I walked around the park, trying to take a perfect shot of the Church, my hiking shoes (the same Merrell hiking shoes I used to walk the Camino de Santiago) crunched the leaves on the ground upon which I walked. Those dried leaves, of course, are already a myriad of beautiful golden hues. As if waking from a dream, I looked around and then suddenly realized how beautiful an Autumn day could be in this fabulous town.

We mingled with tourists in the city for the next couple of days and amused ourselves watching them being herded around. Indeed, the first thing we noticed was the high number of Chinese visitors bringing steady revenues to the several Chinese restaurants in town. There were also many Russians in town, and we met a friendly couple who stayed in the room opposite us. I was informed that the Russians contributed to reconstructing St. Peter and St. Paul church we had just visited. Numerous stalls and shops were selling spouted ceramic drinking cups. We saw many day-trippers strolling along the impressive colonnades, with these spouted ceramic drinking cups in their hands and sipping the sulphurous waters collected from the thermal fountains.

On the morning of the fourth day, we fortified ourselves with a good breakfast and strong tea and resolved to move on like brave soldiers to go anywhere and do anything! I had on hand a Spa Walks guide which we picked up from the Tourist information office. There are many lovely walking trails in the forests surrounding Karlovy Vary. I decided that we should take a mixture of trails leading eventually to Zamecky Virk (Diana). "I hear I forget; I see I remember; I do I understand." As I write this journal, I realized that I had actually "lived" this mixed trail. I knew and understood it retrospectively because of the "impression" it had on me. That "impression", even though less profound than that which the Camino Frances had on me, had the same encouraging introspection, which also led to increased knowledge and understanding of myself. Am I being self-centred or getting a little more spiritual with advancing age? Many years from now, I might be telling this story with a smile. With so many wonderful trails crisscrossing in the woods, I took this one less (perhaps never) travelled by, and that has made all the difference.

"The woods are lovely, dark and deep, But I have promises to keep, And miles to go before I sleep, And miles to go before I sleep." – David Frost

"In many a walk At evening or by moonlight, or reclined At midday upon beds of forest moss, Have we to Nature and her impulses Of our whole being made free gift, and when Our trance had left us, oft have we, by aid Of the impressions which it left behind Looked inward on ourselves, and learned perhaps, something of what we are."- William Wordsworth

SWIEBODZIN POLAND

From Karlovy Vary, we went by train to Nuremberg and Berlin, then travelled eastward again and ended up in Poland. I promised that I would share this story. I like to tell relatives and friends that I want to travel on the road and to places less travelled. One of the amazing things about travelling to non-touristic places is that even with that knowledge I gained from (or through the eyes of) Doctor Google, my expectations would pale in comparison with what would appear before my own eyes. New places that I have never visited always astound me. It changes my perception of the world we live in, with different awe-inspiring sceneries, landscapes, flavours and cultures, the wonderful people (different from us and yet the same) and the good side of them which we never knew. Strangers come into our lives for a reason.

We were lost, and a stranger walked with us and showed us how to get to Berlin Lichtenburg station from where we would take the train to Swiebodzin, a small, unassuming town in Western Poland. A vendor in this small, modest town declined payment from May for her apple. The name of this quiet town, "Swiebodzin", struck me with the sound of "We both sin!."

On our way to the lodging in Swiebodzin, I was struck by the sight of Christ The King, a statue standing majestically on a small hill. We checked into the small hotel nearby. The place looked deserted as we did not see anyone else in the small hotel. Our hostess, who did not speak English, used sign language to show us our room, which was a lovely suite. She managed to convey to us some understanding that she would bring us breakfast the next day, which she did. This is undoubtedly not a tourist-infested place. We walked to the small village town nearby and, after a simple "dinner", retired to the bedroom in our suite. There was a portrait of John Paul II hanging on the wall. This was the first time I stayed in a bedroom with the picture of a Pope!

On my first night in this town, a strange thing happened. On that night, I had a "Field of Dreams" moment too. Many people have misquoted what Shoeless Joe Jackson said. I had built the site: www.freepilgrim.com but have people come? Still, I must write about this journey and share this story because I care. That evening, we decided to rise early the following day to explore Swiebodzin immediately after breakfast on foot. However, when morning broke, we nearly relented our determination because we saw through the window a thick chilly mist. A dark, ominous cloud was forming, and the distant rumblings warned us that a thunderstorm was approaching. Our fitness levels were not ideal, but I suppose for our age, deemed serviceable. However, May's early morning habit is more like that of a Shanghai lady than a Shaolin or that of an Athenian than a Spartan. The only time we both got up this early was we were on the Camino five years ago. Yet, despite the struggle, we managed to catch the early morning crisp air. The opportunity to explore would not arrive for us if we did not take it today. I observed the sky one more time and realized that rain was not imminent. With the hope that the weather would change for the better for us, we continued with our exploration of this least ravelled location in Poland

Along our walk in the neighbourhood, I heard a man lecturing and scolding his dog, barking too loud. This disturbed the peace and joy of the early morning. It displeased him immensely. Indeed, some would deem it cruel to do so as some tendered-hearted thought it a sin to exterminate the flies and mosquitoes and consider it a wee-bit short of murder to kill a snake. Well, there are differences of opinion in this world, and maybe as well there should be! We walked by some houses and saw pomegranates weighing on the branches and a police station with policemen just hanging around without "business" to attend to...and the rain never came

Swiebodzin is an important transportation hub with the A2 and S3 motorways crossing near it. Rail lines run from Berlin, passing through Swiebodzin to Poznan onwards to Warsaw. With its geographical position, the town's population very likely had a mixed Polish and German ancestry, but Germans were the majority by the early modern period. Despite the local conflicts and the turbulent years of the Reformation and Counter-Reformation of the 16th and early 17th centuries, the demographics changed, and the town expanded economically.

The centre still contains remnants of the town's past as a walled settlement. There were two nearly intact towers and fragments of the town's defensive walls and bastions at the time of our visit. The Town Hall, built around 1550 in the renaissance style, dominates the central market square. It was rebuilt in the 19th century with a prominent clock tower that is standing impressively today.

Construction of a giant statue of Christ the King on a hill began in the summer of 2008. It was built on the outskirts of the town and was intended to serve as a site for future pilgrimage. The statue lays claim to be the tallest and largest statue of Jesus. It was completed in November 2010, funded by donations from local people and from people as far away as Canada. It is composed of concrete and fibreglass. Wikipedia provides a helpful chart and list comparing the heights of the world's tallest Christ statues.

Christ The King in Swiebodzin, Poland, which is not so well known as the statue of Christ The Redeemer of Rio de Janeiro (constructed between 1922 and 1931), is listed as the tallest in the world today. It is 32.85 metres with the crown (117.8 ft) and without the crown at 33 metres (108 ft) tall, symbolising a traditional belief that Jesus's age at his death was 33. "By His death he opened to us the way of freedom and peace." On the earthly level, I walked up to the base of the statue. I then and realized that my journey must continue on the spiritual level to get nearer to Christ. I am finishing this journal in preparation to light the fourth (4ᵗʰ) candle of Advent, and Christmas is soon upon us. Just a thought: Perhaps we are still in bondage and need to be freed to find peace and joy in this life. But when we live on the edge in this confusing world, in this uncertain time of cacophony and war of deception, who will set us free? To find joy, we need first to find peace. To find peace, we need to be truly free. "If the Son, therefore, shall make you free, ye shall be free indeed" + John 8:36 (KJV). "Come, walk with me." Together we will walk to The Prince of Peace...Maranatha, Come Jesus come.

The Land of Queen of Sheba

Long ago, as a little boy, I grew up with the story of Tarzan, and later as a young man, I read about Dr Livingstone. Like those interested in adventures in this age and time, I often associate Africa with the "Big 5", four of which (except the leopard) I had seen on safari in South Africa. But I also wanted to know and yearned to experience what this vast continent, three times the size of Canada, was all about if I strip away the "Big 5" and the wildlife-based images which isolate us from the rest of fellow humans and humanity. Enters "The Land of The Queen of Sheba" - Ethiopia - a Christian land long before much of Europe and the rest of the world. Sheba was an ancient realm that existed many centuries before Christ.

Some historians believe that it included what is now modern Ethiopia and Yemen. The realm traded in incense and prospered because of its links with Jerusalem and the Roman Empire. In Jewish legend, the Queen of Sheba was the Queen of Egypt and Ethiopia, and she was said to have brought the first balsam tree to Israel. Muslims refer to the Queen of Sheba as the "queen of the south" with the name of Bilkis. Queen of Sheba is well-known as a Biblical figure even though little is written about her origin. "And she came to Jerusalem with a very great train, with camels that bare spices, and very much gold, and precious stones: and when she was come to Solomon, she communed with him of all that was in her heart." I Kings 10:2 (KJV).

Making the past relevant to the present is what archaeologists have been doing. A team of British archaeologists have recently discovered an enormous gold mine in northern Ethiopia. The excavations have also discovered a temple and, most recently – a large palace. The site is located on the high Gheralta plateau. The archaeologists knew from the 20ft stone stele carved with the image of the sun and crescent moon (the emblem of Sheba) that this was once part of the realm of the Queen. Archaeologist Louise Schofield told The Guardian shortly after the discovery by the British team: "One of the things I've always loved about archaeology is the way it can tie up with legends and myths. The fact that we might have the Queen of Sheba's mines is extraordinary." Professor Brian Cox, on a visit to Ethiopia's Rift Valley (2014), said: "It's impossible to sit here and not catch a glimpse, out of your peripheral vision, of a line of ghosts stretching back 10,000 generations because we're all related to someone from here." ...was he thinking of AL 288-1 "Lucy"?

Ethiopians have good reason to take their history very seriously, and they do. It was one of only two African countries not colonized. It is commonly accepted that the first humans came from the Rift Valley. I was also thinking about AL288-1! Having previously read the article "Lucy Dethroned" by Bert Thompson and Brad Harrub (both PhD) I was determined to see "Lucy" as I stepped into the National Museum of Addis Ababa. But I saw only a replica of Dinkinesh. The real "Lucy", I was informed, is stored in a specially constructed safe in the Paleoanthropology Laboratories.

In the years since "Lucy" was discovered in her 3.2-million-year-old grave, scientists have gone on to find older and even more complete fossil remains of Australopithecus afarensis. In Ethiopia, scientists have unearthed the remains of a 3.3-million-year-old baby dubbed "Selam." This child was 100,000 years older than "Lucy", but it's now often known as "Lucy's Baby." Perhaps even more spectacular was a 4.4-million-year-old Ardipithecus ramidus "Ardi," the earliest known skeleton of a HOMINID. News of "Ardi" first came to light in 1994, but since then, scientists have found evidence of hominids dating back as far as 7 million years ago... Two fossils of an ape-like creature named Graecopithecus Freyberg, which had human-like teeth, have been found in Bulgaria and Greece. The discovery of the creature proves that our "ancestors" were already starting to "evolve" in Europe 200,000 years before the earliest African hominid... these fascinating "evolution" stories continue... Notwithstanding this, Ethiopia is not a country for cynics even if one does not believe in The Kebra Nagast or even the Scripture.

ADDIS ABABA

Addis Ababa (Amharic for "the new flower"), founded only 150 years ago by Menelik II, is now a metropolis of more than 6 million people. It is the country's sprawling capital in the Ethiopian highlands and the country's commercial hub. At an altitude of 2355m, it is one of the highest capitals of the world. It also hosts the headquarters of the United Nations Economic Commission for Africa (ECA) and of the African Union (AU).

Flying into Addis Ababa was exciting for me, but it was also slightly intimidating. I was completely unsure of what to expect as we walked out of the airport. Ethiopia was going to be unlike anywhere else I had seen - and I had not seen anything yet. Having been a traveller and globetrotter for many years, I understand that sometimes things get lost in translation. Sometimes, words or phrases just cannot be converted exactly from one language to the other. It is also not so unusual for countries to have different calendars. But for clocks and time? We arrived in Addis Ababa early in the morning from Toronto and asked our driver from the hotel for the exact time... "It's two o'clock" He chuckled and added, "In Ethiopia." It was actually 8:00 am. I soon discovered that there are two ways to tell the time in Ethiopia. They count time by the 12-hour cycles. It can be confusing for foreigners at first, but we all get it eventually. It is just a matter of time ☺.

Africa is much more Christian than many people realize, and Ethiopia was actually an early cradle of Christianity. The Methane Alem "Saviour of the World" Cathedral (Ethiopian Orthodox) seen from our hotel window is the second-largest cathedral in the whole of Africa and the largest in Ethiopia.

Several years ago, we met some persons by chance as we were walking in one of the lovely parks in Ontario. The strangers asked us whether we knew Lalibela. The name had stuck in my mind ever since. People come into our lives for a reason. Since that encounter with the strangers, I had harboured the desire to visit this place called Lalibela. As we were approaching this Season in our liturgical calendar, I found an opportunity to go for a "retreat" on the foothill of the mountainous region of Ethiopia with Lalibela as the focal point for our "retreat." We would be away for about 20 days at the beginning of Lent and hope to gradually make our way back to Vancouver from Lalibela and Aksum by Laetare Sunday.

BAHIR DAR

On this journey, I discovered the source of the "Blue Nile" - Lake Tana, where even the hippos, pelicans, Cormorants, and others came to say "hello" to us. Lake Tana is close to Bahir Dar, the third-largest city in Ethiopia, after Addis Ababa and Dire Dawa. It is the capital of the Amhara region, inhabited by the Amhara people, the country's ethnically second largest group. The official Ethiopian language is Amharic. Bahir Dar is popular with tourists because of its lake and comfortable climate. It has become the jumping-off point for the Blue Nile Falls and Gondar to Lalibela for those interested in doing the northern historical loop. The main reason for some coming here is also to launch a boat excursion out onto Lake Tana to visit its monasteries.

We berthed at the small jetty on the Zege Peninsula and trekked up the hill on a winding path to visit the Azwa Maryam monastery, where a local tour guide demonstrated to us how a stone is struck to signal meal times at a monastery.

GONDAR

From Bahir Dar, we travelled by road to Gondar, a city located in the Semien Gondar Zone of the Amhara Region. On the way between Bahir Dar and Gondar, we saw the Rocky outcrop or "God's finger."

Gondar is north of Tana Lake on the Lesser Angereb River and southwest of the Simien Mountains. Gondar served as a strong Christian kingdom for many years. It previously served as the capital of both the Ethiopian Empire and still holds the remains of several royal castles, including those in Fasil Ghebbi (the Royal Enclosure), for which Gondar has been called the "Camelot of Africa".

The Royal Enclosure or Fasil Ghebbi is the remains of a fortress-city founded in the 17th century by Emperor Fasilides (Fasil) and was the home of Ethiopia's emperors. Its unique architecture shows diverse influences, including Nubian styles and the site was inscribed as a UNESCO World Heritage Site in 1979.

Encapsulated by tall trees a couple of kilometres northwest of the piazza lies Fasiladas' Bath. The large rectangular pool overlooked by a charming building was likely to have been constructed for religious celebrations, the likes of which still go on today. It is in a serene spot and peaceful spot where snakelike tree roots encircle sections of the stone walls like what I saw at Ta Prohm in Angkor Wat.

Although there was no water in the Bath during our visit, I was told that once a year, the Bath is filled with water for the Timket celebration (the Orthodox Tewahedo celebration of Epiphany). During "Timket", the city would be inundated with pilgrims who come to re-enact the baptism of Jesus in the River Jordan and take a dip in the holy waters (after being blessed by the bishop) at the historical Fasilides Bath. The ceremony replicates Christ's baptism in the Jordan River and is seen as an important renewal of faith.

TO LALIBELA

Exploring Ethiopia is like stepping into the pages of the Old Testament. Ancient religious treasures are abundant. The medieval monuments here – many are UNESCO World Heritage Sites – including the island monasteries of Lake Tana and the rock-hewn Churches of Lalibela are some of the world's finest. From Gondar, we flew into the historic town of Lalibela. Early Christian architecture in Ethiopia is reflected in the 11 rock-hewn churches of Lalibela. The most complete monolithic church is the Church of St. George (Bet Giyorgis), which looks like a cross when seen from above.

The 11 rock-hewn churches were not constructed from the ground up but chiselled out of the red volcanic rock hills instead. The churches were built in the 13th century on the orders of King Lalibela as the "New Jerusalem" after Muslim forces overran the Holy City. The churches were constructed around Ethiopia's own stretch of the "Jordan River." Legend has it that the thousands of labourers who toiled on Lalibela's "New Jerusalem" by day were helped by angels who continued the work by night. Lalibela is understandably a place o f pilgrimage.

We ventured further out into the countryside. We hiked up to an altitude of 2800m on the west side of Mount Abuna Yosef mountain to view the cave church of " Yemrehanna Kristos". Mural paintings high on the nave walls of the church are considered the oldest surviving mural paintings in Ethiopia

AKSUM OR AXUM

We arrived at Aksum, a city in northern Ethiopia known for its obelisks, the relics of the ancient Kingdom. Most are still standing in the Northern Stelae Park. The tallest of the monoliths, fallen and broken into six massive pieces, was 33.3 meters tall and weighed an estimated five tons. These obelisks (also called stelae) are known to be the tallest single pieces of stone ever quarried and erected in the ancient world. Their age and use remain a complete mystery.

Some coins found at the base of these giant pillars suggest to some scholars that they may have been carved and erected around the beginning of the 4th century AD. The stelae were carved from solid blocks of nepheline syenite, similar in appearance to granite believed to have come from the quarries of Wuchate Golo several miles to the west of Aksum. This group of seven stelae was erected around the same time of tremendous change in Aksumite culture when the Aksum's court adopted Christianity. It has been suggested that the failure to erect the largest stelae (which cracked and fell into pieces) while being installed might have accelerated the adoption of the new religion of Christianity. In any event case, these stelae were the last to have been dedicated to Aksum.

The Axumite king Ezana was converted to Christianity In 331 AD by the Syrian monk Frumentius. Consequently, the church of St. Mary (perhaps the earliest Christian church in sub-Saharan Africa) is believed to have been built during his reign. The church was destroyed and has been rebuilt several times since. Its first putative destruction occurred at the hands of Queen Gudit during the 10th century. Its second confirmed destruction occurred in the 16th century at the hands of Ahmad ibn Ibrahim al-Ghazi. Emperor Gelawdewos rebuilt it, then further rebuilt and enlarged it by Fasilides during the 17th century. The old church remains accessible only to men.

Nearby is the Chapel of the Tablet adjacent to the old church, which contains the Ark of The Covenant. According to tradition, the Ark came to Ethiopia with Menelik I (the son of Solomon and the Queen of Sheba) after he visited his father, King Solomon. It became clear to me that this veneration of the church was born from a belief that God has chosen this site as the final resting place of the Ark of the Covenant.

The Ark of the Covenant still plays a significant role in the consciousness and belief of the Christians that dominate the Ethiopian population. This is a society with profound Christian spirituality where worship is woven into nearly every aspect of life. Many of the Christians we came across were fasting. Fasting, prayers chanting, and daily celebrations (which we could hear from wherever we stayed) were vivid expressions of their spirituality that built these communities of faith. They have preserved a strong sense of history and tradition, and I believe that through their tradition, spirituality, rich liturgy, and mystical theology, they can make a unique contribution to Christianity as a whole.

Ethiopia was introduced to the Christian faith by the Ethiopian eunuch, who was baptized by the apostle Philip. He was the first Ethiopian converted in Jerusalem: "And he arose and went: and, behold, a man of Ethiopia, a eunuch of great authority under Candace queen of the Ethiopians, who had the charge of all her treasure, and had come to Jerusalem for to worship." - Acts 8:27-39 (KJV). Ethiopia was further Christianized in 4 AD by two men, most likely brothers from Tyre (now in Lebanon). Frumentius and Christianity baptized the Aksumite King Ezana were then made the state religion.

In the 1950s, Emperor Haile Selassie ordered the construction of a new modern Cathedral (Byzantine Revival Architecture -style) that was open to both men and women next to the old Cathedral of Our Lady Mary of Zion. Today we saw women processing and entering the church. I believe and understand (as we seek God in our own way) that here, as they seek God with their whole hearts and souls, will find Him.

TIYA AND ADADI MARYAM

After coming back to Addis Ababa from Aksum, we had a couple of days to spare before our flight home to Vancouver. Somehow, I had a feeling that our journey to this intriguing country would not be complete without a visit to the south. We were advised that King Lalibela had commissioned the construction of a church during his visit to the southern region of Shewa. The church Adadi Mariam is a rock-hewn monolithic church (like those in Lalibela though less grand) located approximately 66 km southwest of Addis Ababa. I was informed that according to Oral traditions, the Adadi Mariam church was established in relation to the coming of Abune Gabre Menfes Qedus, one of the most prominent saints of the Ethiopian Orthodox Tewahido Church.

This rock-hewn church is an old sanctuary in the building tradition of the northern part of Ethiopia and marked the advent of Christianity in the southern part of the country. Both man-made and natural causes have damaged the church over time. Restoration work to strengthen and restore the church has been done recently with the aid of Switzerland.

Tiya is in the Soddo Region of Ethiopia, south of Addis Ababa. On our way to Adadi Maryam, we had the opportunity to visit the UNESCO World Heritage Site remarkable for its stelae which are engraved with enigmatic symbols, notably swords.

The archaeological site was designated a World Heritage Site in 1980. Archaeologists appeared to have abandoned the research at Tiya as there are several difficulties in understanding these types of sites from an archaeological standpoint. I was informed that it is difficult to determine the megalith builders' identity and reconstruct ethnic histories through oral historical accounts that are unavailable or uninformative. It makes me wonder whether this has anything to do with Queen Gudit, the non-Christian queen (Ref: Gudit Stelae Field, Axum) who laid waste to Axum and its countryside, destroyed churches and monuments, and attempted to exterminate the members of the ruling dynasty of the Kingdom of Aksum.

On our way back from Tiya to Addis Ababa, we came across hundreds of people near an orthodox church, and our guide indicated to us that they were attending a funeral. Funerals are a big affair in Ethiopia, which follow strict religious customs. I learned that after the funeral, there is a procession and gathering at the burial location, usually near a church or cemetery and that rather than being a small ceremony for close family, an Ethiopian funeral is typically a large, community-wide event. As many as 1,000 people at the funeral accounted for the multitude of people we saw.

PEACE AND HOPE

Ethiopia and Eritrea, two of the world's poorest countries, spent hundreds of millions of dollars on the war between 1998-2000 and suffered tens of thousands of casualties as a direct consequence of the conflict. Eritrea broke international law and triggered the war by invading Ethiopia - a ruling by an international commission in The Hague. A Peace Agreement was finally signed on July 9 2018, the year before our visit. Ethiopia (despite being one of the fastest growing economies) in terms of GDP per capita still at the time of our visit scores among the lowest in the World.

However, according to the latest International Monetary Fund (IMF) Economic Outlook for Africa, Ethiopia's economy is forecast to grow 8.5% this Ethiopian fiscal year, which ends on 7th July 2019. The International Monetary Fund has praised Ethiopia's remarkable progress over more than a decade, which has led to a significant reduction in poverty and improved living standards for many Ethiopians. Although we stay here in relative comfort, it is humbling to realize how privileged we are as we witness such abject poverty. At the same time, it was pure joy to cross paths with some friendly Ethiopians interested in why we are here, what we do and our way of life in affluent Canada. Some obviously want to know more about life than the life they know!

Just a thought: As we waded into the market chaos of the Merkato, west of Addis' centre, it dawned on me that despite the surrounding conditions and poverty, we did not come across any panhandlers or beggars; everyone seemingly was working awfully hard...God bless them!

"10 For even when we were with you, this we commanded you, that if any would not work, neither should he eat. 11 For we hear that there are some which walk among you disorderly, working not at all, but are busybodies. 12 Now them that are such we command and exhort by our Lord Jesus Christ, that with quietness they work, and eat their own bread."- 2 Thessalonians 3:10-12 (KJV).

Journey to Transylvania and beyond

When you think of the big European cities that people tend to visit, you get these familiar names: Amsterdam, Barcelona, Copenhagen, Frankfurt, London, Paris, and Rome. Krakow, Poland's second-largest city and former capital, barely gets a mention. I decided to visit Krakow and journey from there to Slovakia and onwards to Romania to get a glimpse of old central and South-Eastern Europe. We took a flight from Vancouver to Warsaw via Toronto.

When we got into our Ab&b in Warsaw that night, a "light bulb" appeared above my head. It dawned on me that I needed to be "educated" to get a clearer picture of Central Europe. It has been nearly 30 years since Poland and the rest of this part of Europe got out of communism, and moreover, it was also occupied by the Nazi during WWII. We can say that Poland has had a rich and dramatic past! As of today, Poland is still being overlooked by North American tourists, perhaps because we still harbour the antiquated belief that Central and Eastern Europe is somehow behind the times...but look...

A new law in Poland was signed at the beginning of 2018, limiting shop openings to the first and last Sunday of the month. By2020, even these are planned to be phased out. Supporters of the ban say that it would benefit workers and their families. There have been some religious reasons for opposing Sunday labour as well. The Poles are Catholic; most still attend church regularly, as I discovered on my recent visits to Sweibodzin and Poznan. They have maintained their churches very well, and the insides are incredibly beautiful. I realized that I had been going to church only as a cultural Christian all of my life. I found myself in church on Sunday because it was Sunday. I had been holding and feeling only the tail of this massive elephant called "Christianity." I was hesitant whether to bow at the altar or genuflect when visiting other distant churches and cathedrals around the world.

After paying a visit to the All-Saints Cathedral, we proceeded to the Old Town. I discovered that when famous Polish composer Frederic Chopin died, at the early age of 39 of tuberculosis in Paris, his sister had his heart removed and preserved. It was moved to Warsaw during the rule of Imperial Russia. The Nazis allowed Chopin's heart to be put in safekeeping during the Warsaw Uprising, and since 1945 it has remained in a crypt at the Holy Cross Church in Warsaw.

I like to see and observe change. My abiding love of history, cultural change and what had gone before such cultural change has carried over into my travels around the world. We stayed in Warsaw for a week and then took a bus to Krakow. I discovered that when a city has been around for as long as Krakow has, there would be plenty of interesting things to see besides cobbled-stone streets and well-planned squares surrounded by ornate buildings.

There are many impressive churches in Krakow, including St. Peter and St. Paul's church, in which the parents of Pope John Paul II were married. St. Peter and St Paul's was also the venue for the Golden Classical Music Concert performed by the orchestra of Saint Maurice (with the best classics comprising of Chopin, Mozart, Schubert, Tchaikovsky, and Vivaldi) when we were there. We had the pleasure of attending.

During our stay in Krakow, we also took the opportunity to visit the Wieliczka Salt Mine, a UNESCO World Heritage site. This labyrinth was filled with intricate salt carvings, including a giant replica of da Vinci's Last Supper on the walls. Our tour guide encouraged us to lick the walls to confirm that it is all salt. Nobody (in our group) did, but I relished the opportunity, tasted it, and confirmed that it was salt indeed! It was probably 6000 years old!

AUSCHWITZ-BIRKENAU

The Auschwitz-Birkenau Concentration Camp was the focal point of our visit to Krakow. The authentic Memorial consists of two parts of the former Nazi camp- Auschwitz and Birkenau. The museum attracts millions of visitors per year. Most people (except Holocaust deniers) understand that Auschwitz is a symbol of terror and genocide. It was established by Nazi Germany in 1940 in the suburbs of Oswiecim a city that was annexed to the Third Reich. It is situated about 50 kilometres west of Krakow. The increasing mass arrests of the political opponents and Jews were beyond the capacity of existing local prisons where they were arrested. Therefore, the reason for the establishment of the camp. The first transport of prisoners reached Auschwitz from Tarnow prison on June 14, 1940.

The statistics are sobering. Most of the estimated 1.3 million arrested were sent to the gas chambers. Others died of starvations and other causes. Krakow has had more than its share of misery and tragedies. Yet, I believe this has resolved to make the city stronger, resilient and in a way more endearing to visitors. A visit to Auschwitz was sombre and thought-provoking for me. I found it a valuable place to reflect and learn, not only about history but, perhaps even more so, something about ourselves and humanity.

SLOVAKIA

Most people would fly into the capital Bratislava when they intended to visit Slovakia. However, we took a Flixbus from Krakow to Kosice, a university town that is much more off the beaten path in the eastern part of the country. I had used this transport company before, travelling from Prague to Dresden and found it reliable and satisfactory. The buses are equipped with comfortable seats, toilet, free Wi-Fi, and power outlets.

The journey from Krakow to Kosice took us about five hours. Kosice grew up on the crossroads of the long-distance merchant roads which connect Eastern Europe with the West and the Baltic with the Black Sea. The settlement existed since the Palaeolithic Age. I surmised that the town plan concept of the town was probably the oldest, the largest and the most preserved among Slovakian towns. I found it quite easy to read and remember the street network. The town's network was basically formed by the three streets, aiming, from the North to the South, with the middle one gradually widened into the shape of a lens. We strolled along the Hlavna Ulica (Main Street) in the architecturally impressive historic centre of Kosice with no fixed destination in mind. This was a splendid morning, with a slight haze and the promise of a fine Autumn day in Kosice. The Pedestrian-only promenade stretched for about 1.2 kilometres. To me, this was a showcase of Gothic, Renaissance, Baroque and Art Nouveau masterpieces.

I admired the majestic facade of St. Elisabeth Cathedral, which dates to 1380. It is the largest church in Slovakia and one of the eastern-most Gothic cathedrals in Europe. According to archaeological and historical sources, the present-day cathedral was built on the ground of an earlier church which was also consecrated to St Elisabeth of Hungary. We decided to pay the Cathedral a visit. May put on her head scarf, and I removed my baseball cap as we approached the main entrance of the Cathedral. The very moment as we entered the Cathedral, I recalled the verse "Be still and know that I am God." Perhaps I have been raised in (and have visited) churches with the "Let All Mortal Flesh Keep Silent" sense of the holy. I love the sense of the holy in places like this. Silence touches that deep part of my soul that words sometimes seem not to able to do.

During my globetrotting and wandering, I have seen a lot of churches and cathedrals (like the Burgos and Leon Cathedrals), but to me, the Elizabeth Cathedral in Kosice contained some of the finest Gothic stained glass to be found anywhere. The stained glass was gorgeous but, at the same time, not gaudy. It possessed wonderfully translucent and iridescent qualities. I looked carefully at the glass against the bright sky and was mesmerized by its richness and colourful transparency. It left me wondering whether that such glass had never been made before, has never been made since and will never be made again in the future...We remained quiet for most of the time in this hushed church where motive candles flickered before wooden saints. In a strange way, I had the feeling that this was also my church as I felt a primal connection with the Christian heritage and tradition.

At the time of our visit the interior (with the many altars, paintings, and wall frescoes) was free for visitors to admire. The main altar dedicated to St. Elizabeth, crafted in 1474–77, consists of two pairs of decorated "wings" with each containing six Gothic paintings that are adjoined to the central part. There are 48 paintings in three themes - Elizabethan, the Passion, and the Advent. After spending some time in the Cathedral, we stepped outside and continued our stroll once again in the shadow of the aristocratic palaces and stately houses. That evening we went out again to enjoy the illuminated splendour of this Cathedral...

There were tourists and locals sitting in the restaurants and cafes admiring the elegant scenery and watching people and the world go by. I observed them for a while and then realized that this was not usually the way I like to visit a country. If I have the choice, I would like to visit at least three separate locations, as I did with Poland, to get a better idea of the country. But sometimes, we just do not have the time or opportunity. I would love to return to Slovakia and see more. With a heavy heart, we bid farewell to Kosice and took the Flixbus to Budapest. From Budapest, we managed to catch the night from the Keleti train station to Brasov.

TO ROMANIA

Brasov

Bound on the east and south by The Carpathian mountain range, which formed its natural borders, Transylvania extended westward to the Apuseni Mountains. It is a historical region located in central Romania. The term Transylvania sometimes encompasses not only Transylvania proper, but also parts of the historical regions of Crişana and Maramureş, and occasionally the Romanian part of Banat. The region is known for the scenery of its Carpathian landscape and its rich history. The Western world commonly associates Transylvania with vampires because of the influence of Bram Stoker's novel "Dracula" and the many Hollywood horror films adaptations. The novelist had a specific location in mind for the Dracula Castle while writing the narrative: an empty mountain top in the Transylvanian Kelemen Alps near the former border with

Moldova. However, I was informed that Bram Stoker never visited Romania. He depicted the imaginary Dracula's castle based upon a description of Bran Castle that was available to him in Britain at the turn of the century. Stoker was purported to have used the illustration of Bran Castle in Charles Boner's book, "Transylvania: Its Product and Its People" (London: Longmans, 1865), to describe his imaginary Dracula's Castle. There were so many amazing places to visit in Brasov, and yet Brasov seemed not to have captured the full attention of travellers planning European trips. We spent a week in Brasov Old Town and learned of its origins and role as an important market town in medieval Transylvania. There was a tale to unravel the secrets of each site we visited. The beautiful cobblestone lane (Strada Sforii) and the colourful houses grabbed my attention, but they looked nothing like the images in my mind of a place where the legend of Count Dracula began.

We visited the Black Church, a German-Evangelical church, one of the celebrated landmark of Brasov and perhaps also one of Eastern and Central Europe's most iconic monuments. The name of the Church was given after the catastrophic fire of 1689 that blackened its wall when the entire city was practically burned down. The church and its surrounding somehow strangely brought forth an image of events that shaped the past of Transylvania. The image of war and peace, from the many foreign invasions to the role of the Saxons who colonised the land and the impact of the Reformation on their society. Nowadays, the church preserves only three of the original six bells that existed. I was informed that here within the church lay the largest collection of Oriental carpets outside Turkey. The altar is one of the oldest in Transylvania. The pulpit, which dates from 1696, is decorated with the sculptures of Moses, the four Evangelists in Christian tradition Matthew, Mark, Luke, and John. From around the same period dates, the mural painting representing Virgin Mary.

We Continued our journey to St Nicholas Church, situated in the Unirii Square in the Schei district of Brasov. The main tower and the two smaller towers of the Church immediately caught my eyes like the charming buildings in fairy tales. It dated to the 15th century and was built on the site of an older church dated around 1292. It was initially built in the Gothic style and later redecorated with architectural elements of Baroque style. Within the courtyard is the Museum of the First Romanian School. I believe St. Nicholas Church, throughout its history, together with the adjacent First Romanian school, had provided the needed religious, spiritual, intellectual, and cultural support to the divers' population of this city.

We spent a week in Brasov, walking on some of the fascinating trails around the city, embracing the majesty of the ancient walls and fortifications amidst its beautiful natural environment.

No visit to Brasov would be complete without a visit to Bran Castle, but we were disappointed that Count Dracula did not show us his lodging. The widely believed connection between Bran Castle and the Dracula legend (of Vlad III Dracula and Bram Stoker's novel) is helpful for tourism purpose.

BUCHAREST

Bucharest, the capital of Romania, for us from Brasov, was just a short ride away. Most visitors to Bucharest would treat the city, unlike the way which we did. They would arrive at the capital, pass through it briefly and head to the northern towns of Transylvania to see, among other sites, the Pele Castle. This Neo-Renaissance castle was built between 1873 and 1914 in the enchanted forest of the Carpathian Mountains on an existing medieval route linking Transylvania and Wallachia. We, unlike most tourists, came from the other direction. However, regardless of which direction we came, we all had to walk up to the end of a beautiful forest path to get the first glimpse of this spectacular Castle set on top of a hill. Despite the glare of the Romanian autumn sun, I removed my "shade" to really appreciate its beauty and majesty which are so fully displayed amidst the colourful foliage.

I had the strong suspicion that many tourists had counted Romania as a visited country but had not, from the cultural perspective, really gathered anything of value. We intended to stay for a while and hoped to immerse ourselves in the rich culture of this fascinating country. But what did I do on this first trip to Bucharest? I rented an Ab&b in Bucharest's Centre, Centrul Vechi, to the locals. Centrul Vechi is the legendary birthplace of Bucharest. It is also Bucharest's unrivalled district for restaurants, cafés, and bars. I discovered that it is a city of contrasts. The design styles stimulated me to the size of buildings and the people we encountered. We saw rooftop bars hosted by century-old buildings, with many boasting beautiful facades and decorations. Just like elsewhere in Central Europe, Bucharest is also about the cafes. People go in the morning or afternoon for coffee, and by nightfall, they have switched to beer and wine.

We wanted to have coffee at the Artichoke Coffee Shop, where I would have had the opportunity to watch and "study" the patrons of the shop. While we were still undecided, a honeybee was circling around me, driving me crazy and making it difficult for me even to take proper photographs. May walked over to the shop called "Libraria Humanitas."

I had a short conversation with one of the patrons who asked me whether I had been able to see Bucharest through the eyes of the homeless and heard the story about Gheorghe. It appeared that Gheorghe was a drug addict who had was homeless in Bucharest for many years and lost many of his friends to drugs. The patron told me that eventually, a local NGO called the Parada Foundation (that gets children off the streets) helped him climb out of homelessness and build a life. The story reminded me of the "complicity" in the problem of Vancouver's Downtown East side. It is complicated!

Bucharest is covered with parks - something that I did not expect in an Eastern European city. It is one of the greenest major cities I have come across in Europe. But I also wanted to take one step further than parks. As a city in a continuous transformation since the fall of Communism, I discovered that Bucharest is probably "cooler" today than the years before. So, I produced the ultimate checklist (while indulging ourselves in some fun) of some of the quirky, creative, and intriguing things and places to visit and see in Bucharest.

Apart from all the "strange" sites, we also saw The Palace of the Parliament, which has a developed area of 365,000 m2, making it the third-largest administrative building globally after The Pentagon and Long'ao Building. I am informed that The Palace of the Parliament is also the heaviest building in the world, weighing about 4,098,500,000 kilograms. Romanian specialists who analyzed the data argue that the massive weight and structure of the Palace lead to the further settlement below the construction, making it sinks by 6 mm each year.

It is left for travellers to discover Bucharest and much more. But we can discover "much more" only if we can "re-educate" ourselves to listen, see and feel what is around us...

From Bucharest, we took the train and continued with our journey towards Sofia in Bulgaria and beyond. My innate ability to listen, seeing and touching no longer comes naturally since I became an adult. The vision and imagination which we once had as little children, destroyed by liberal schoolings, harmful cacophony of the modern society and popular culture, must be rediscovered.

I have learned from Thomas Merton that most of our senses need to be educated (re-educated?) for us to listen and see and appreciate what surround us. I remember the tea ceremony performed by our son Nigel and his bride Haruna at their wedding reception. In the Eastern tradition of tea ceremony, every individual is greeted with respect and courtesy. The things (tea utensils, cups, saucers, and a tray laid out in order) were handled with care, and the tea served according to tradition in such an orderly way as if to pay homage to the contributions they each play in the event. This simple tea ceremony demonstrated the sensitive feeling of respect and reverence for both people and things, like what I found so common in the Benedictine Way.

We must be constantly reminded that progress is not always all gain. It is not necessarily so. St. Paul advises us "to hold fast that which is good." Beauty and good will not come to us at all if they do not come into the correct perspective. Beauty and the good of the past, once gone, is irrecoverable.

The Lands Of Transformation

BULGARIA

I told my relatives and friends that I would be travelling across the "ia" countries. The "ia" countries were Slovakia, Romania, Bulgaria, Macedonia, and Albania. These were all former communist countries in the European continent. I have already been to Croatia, Slovenia, and the Czech Republic (former Czechoslovakia). On 1 January 1993, Czechoslovakia separated peacefully (in what is known as "velvet divorce") into two new countries becoming the Czech Republic and Slovakia.

For this journey, I would leave aside three other "ia" countries - Serbia, Armenia, and Bosnia (Herzegovina). But what really is Eastern Europe? Several definitions of Eastern Europe exist today, depending on the context in which they are used. They are lacking in precision and are outdated. The "boundaries" of Eastern Europe are subject to overlap and fluctuations. The definitions vary among experts, even among political scientists, as the term "Eastern Europe" has a wide range of geographical, socio-economic, and cultural connotations. In many cases, regions are social constructs defined by abstract, neutral criteria and not necessarily strict physical features. Therefore, there are "almost as many definitions of Eastern Europe as there are scholars of the region". A United Nations paper adds that "every assessment of spatial identities is essentially a social and cultural construct."

Background

On a previous journey of ours from Athens to Northern Greece, we came across some Greeks in a Chinese restaurant in Thessaloniki. We were pleasantly surprised to hear them speaking fluent Mandarin Chinese. We got into a spirited conversation with them and discovered that they were Christian missionaries. They were trying to share the good news of the Gospel (Evangelion) with the Chinese population. I like to think that as true believers and followers of Jesus, they did not believe they were offending the spirituality of the Chinese (if there is such) in carrying out the instruction of the Risen Christ :-(Mathew 28:19). This was where we were witnessing the parakletos at work in the transformation of the beings. People come into our lives for a reason. On a lighter note, we were also advised by them to visit Bulgaria, a short drive from Thessaloniki, if ever we find the opportunity to do so.

Three years later, May and I found the opportunity to do so. Here we are, on our way to Bulgaria (albeit) from the other direction – from Romania... In planning for this journey, I was aware that while the eastern geographical boundaries of Europe are quite well defined, the boundary between Eastern and Western Europe is not geographical but historical, religious, and cultural. However, I will treat Bulgaria, Macedonia and Albania as falling within the confine of South-Eastern Europe. These countries were under Communist rule – People's Republic of Bulgaria (1946–1991), Socialist Republic of Macedonia (1945–1991) and People's Socialist Republic of Albania (1946–1992).

I was informed that it was impossible for people to practice their religion under communist systems, and there were some religious persecutions in these countries. Communism does not recognise a god, as does Christianity. Marxism sees individuals as the creators of their own environment. In Christianity, God is the creator. These two different world views created tension. Although there was some freedom of religion in these countries (Albania being the exception at that time), there were restrictions on religious expression in practice.

During the Cold War period, religious practices and church activities were regulated and closely monitored. Churches invariably found themselves in very precarious positions. Communist rule was to erase the church as an institution. In some cases, this was successful. But even in their restricted position, churches had played a significant role as proponents of change. Some historians believe that communist governments underestimated the dynamics and significance of Christianity.

According to researcher Dr Katharina Kunter, even though in the political context of the Cold War (where every country in Eastern Europe had its own special characteristics), the ecumenical contacts between Christian churches helped them to reimagine Christianity as a multinational movement. This generated an especially important sense of solidarity under communist rule and during the Cold War. The spiritual and pastoral duties of the churches also received much attention. Between years 1989-1992, opposition to totalitarian communism became very visible. Communism in Eastern Europe finally collapsed.

After the fall of communism, the new political elites were faced with the challenges of creating the institutions of democracy: the transformation of state-planned economies into market economies, the gradual introduction of the rule of law, and civil society's growth. It was not clear that these former communist countries would be able to transform themselves successfully.

We arrived in Bulgaria from Romania by train on October 15th, 2019. We left Bucharest North station (Romania) at 12:40 with one change at Russe and arrived in Sofia (Bulgaria) at 22:20. This train journey took us through some incredible sceneries as we crossed the Danube (which separated Romania and Bulgaria) over one of the longest steel bridges in Europe. The Romania-Bulgaria border is an internal border of the European Union. At the time of our visit, neither Romania nor Bulgaria is part of the Schengen area. In consequence of this, border controls are conducted between the two countries. We waited in the comfort of our compartment for border officials to collect our passports, stamped and returned to us

After we checked into our Ab&b that evening, I recalled our conversation with the Greek Missionaries at Thessaloniki. I did a search on Religions in Bulgaria and discovered that in concert with the fall of communism in Bulgaria, Christianity has also seen a decline, with the most serious from 2001 onwards. According to the 2011 censor, the percentage of Christians in the overall population has dropped from 86.6% in 1992 to 61% in 2011. However, unlike former Yugoslavia (in the 1990s), Bulgaria has not experienced any significant ethnic or religious confrontations. I observed and had the comfortable feeling that the religious communities in this country could coexist peacefully.

Our Ab&b was close to Vitosha Boulevard, the main pedestrian street in Sofia. It is a walking boulevard "claimed" by the pedestrians for cosmopolitan dining with varied Greek French Italian Chinese Arab & of course local menu to offer. This street is "alive", and it was interesting for us to take our daily walk there. We also took the advice of someone we met and so ventured further out to a tiny café called the Mekitsa & Coffee. There we saw a selection of the mekitsas (fried dough) topped with a variety of either sweet or savoury toppings. We tried the traditional mekitsa with powdered sugar and one with a blend of cheese.

But there are more to see in Bulgaria, especially in the old town in Plovdiv. Plovdiv remains relatively unknown to most North American tourists, but it is being featured on increasingly Balkan itineraries - for good reason. At the time of our visit, it has already been declared the European Capital of Culture 2019. A lady of Bulgarian heritage, with her Scottish husband, has recently become our "neighbours" in Vancouver. She had advised me that the Old City of Plovdiv is a must-visit if I ever decide to travel to Bulgaria. I took her advice as I am a dilettante in observing the process of change and transformation. In visiting old cities around the world (especially old city like Plovdiv), I would be fascinated by the designs and constructions formed because of continued human habitation, combining cultures and architectures of different periods, from Antiquity, Middle Ages, and revival to the modern age. Plovdiv has a strong claim to being the oldest continually inhabited city in Europe. With its winding cobbled streets and elegant revival-era townhouses, the old town was a perfect place for us to have our leisurely afternoon stroll.

165

The Greeks, Romans, Byzantines, and the Turks have all fought to claim Plovdiv as their own. Plovdiv was originally established by the Thracians around 5000 BC. It is difficult to summarize 7000 years of visible history of this old city. We saw the Roman stadium and the partially unearthed stadium below the main street. A short distance from the Roman Stadium the 600-year-old Dzhumaya Mosque still serves the Muslim Turkish families who stayed behind after the collapse of Ottoman rule.

MACEDONIA

Someone who is well-informed would ask me which Macedonia I would visit. That would be a legitimate question. I was interested in visiting Skopje, so that would be the Republic of North Macedonia, a successor state of the former Yugoslavia. This country became a member of the United Nations in April 1993, but there had been a dispute with Greece over the name "Macedonia". It is significant to note that the nationality of Alexander the Great was one of the issues that had fed into the dispute between Greece and the Former Yugoslav Republic of Macedonia (FYROM) over the name. Alexander the Great was born in July 365 BCE in Pella, the capital of Ancient Macedonia, which now sits within modern Greece. The conflict was resolved between Macedonia and Greece, barely a year before our visit, agreeing that the country be renamed "Republic of North Macedonia." This renaming came into effect in February 2019. So, here we were, visiting a new country and an old country with a new name. Skopje, the capital and the largest city of North Macedonia, is the country's political, cultural, economic, and academic centre.

This will be my visit to the fourth country among the six socialist republics in the former Socialist Federal Republic of Yugoslavia (SFRY with Belgrade as its capital) consisting of Bosnia and Herzegovina, Croatia, Macedonia, Montenegro, Serbia, and Slovenia. with Belgrade as its capital) consisting of Bosnia and Herzegovina, Croatia, Macedonia, Montenegro, Serbia, and Slovenia.

Even though Skopje has been destroyed many times throughout its history, there are still many historical landmarks that reflect the city's successive occupations. Skopje has one of the biggest Ottoman urban complexes in Europe, with many Ottoman monuments still serving their original purpose. We decided to visit The Old Bazaar, one of the oldest and largest marketplaces in the Balkans. The earliest known sources which mentioned its existence date back to the 12th century.

Under the Ottoman, the Old Bazaar developed rapidly to become the city's main centre of commerce. The Ottoman history of the bazaar is evidenced by the mosques, numerous caravanserais, and Hans (Turkish for 'Lead Inn'), which we saw among other buildings and monuments. We soon discovered that inside the Old Bazaar was a maze of oddly shaped blocks of shop houses and covered market areas lining the sides of narrow stone alleys that occasionally open out into slightly wider streets and public squares. The bazaar was heavily damaged by earthquakes that occurred in 1555 and 1963 and during the First and the Second World Wars. However, since the earthquake of 1963, it has become a ground for creative and modernist experiments. At the time of our visit, I noticed that it is once again the subject of massive building campaigns, due to project "Skopje 2014".

As part of the Yugoslav Wars, North Macedonia did experience some violence in 2001, but it did not reach the level of violence experienced in other countries such as Bosnia and Herzegovina, and the conflict was predominantly ethnic, rather than religious, in character. I was informed by people we came across that Skopje is a city where old, reactionary, eastern, and western perspectives coexist, even though incidences of vandalism have occurred at some religious sites. The Macedonian Orthodox Church has reported acts of vandalism of Orthodox churches, including an attempt in February 2017 to burn the door of a church in Saraj. Pew Research Center estimates that Christians will fall to 55.1% of the country's population due to meagre fertility rates. Perhaps it is good that they have recently constructed the Millennium Cross as a memorial for 2,000 years of Christianity in the region.

Saint Paul began spreading Christianity in Macedonia towards the mid 1st century AD. "And a vision appeared to Paul in the night; There stood a man of Macedonia, and prayed him, saying, come over into Macedonia, and help us. And after he had seen the vision, immediately we endeavoured to go into Macedonia, assuredly gathering that the Lord had called us for to preach the gospel unto them.": -Acts 16 :9-10 (KJV).

He visited Berea during his journeys through Europe and Asia. Berea or Beroea was a city of the Hellenic and Roman era now known as Veria (or Veroia) in Macedonia, northern Greece. This town Berea (in Macedonia) is mentioned in the Acts of the Apostles, where the apostles Paul (followed by Timothy and Silas) preached the Christian gospel. "And the brethren immediately sent away Paul and Silas by night unto Berea: who coming thither went into the synagogue of the Jews. These were more noble than those in Thessalonica, in that they received the word with all readiness of mind, and searched the scriptures daily, whether those things were so." Acts 17 :10-11 (KJV).

We visited the newly consecrated Church of Saint Clement of Ohrid, a rotunda type church composing of domes and arches. It is an interesting Macedonian architectural design, and at the time of our visit, the largest cathedral of the Macedonian Orthodox Church. The construction of the cathedral began in 1972 and was consecrated in 1990 on the 1150th anniversary of the birth of the church patron saint, St. Clement of Ohrid. The main church is dedicated to St. Clement of Ohrid, and one of the chapels is dedicated to Emperor Constantine and Empress Helena.

Less than an hour by car from the city, we found yourselves at the very gate to the Macedonian countryside. We arrived at a nature paradise known as Canyon Matka, an outdoor attraction covering 5000 hectares of breathtaking scenery. However, it is nonetheless ignored or unknown by many. Canyon Matka is relatively underrated even though it is easily one of the most captivating places we came across on this journey.

On the way back from Matka Canyon, we visited a small 12th-century Byzantine church located in a monastery complex. The church was constructed in 1164 with irregularly shaped stone blocks and bricks embedded in layers of mortar. I was fascinated by the Byzantine art frescoes inside the church depicting scenes from the Passion of Christ and various hagiographies. I felt the sanctitude of this simple church. I have always known and fully understand that each one of us has individual consciousness of the things around us, and different people are affected differently (if at all) when they visit places such as this. Christian traditions concerning such places point to a mystery that neither theologians nor the scientific community have yet been able to explain.

There were so many things to see, taste, feel, and touch in North Macedonia, but we had to move on. So, the next day we left Skopje on a mini-coach for Albania

ALBANIA

Many of us do not realize that despite the spread of Christianity in this part of the world by the early church, the commonly practised religion in Albania is Islam (mainly Sunni or Bektashi). Christianity comes second (mainly Orthodox and Catholic). There are also many irreligious people. In a sense, Albania is "neutral in questions of belief and conscience" and constitutionally a secular country since 1967. The Marxist-Leninist government from 1946 to 1992 declared Albania as the world's first and only "Atheist state". But after the end of its communist regime.

In 1991 and years of severe religious persecution, The Orthodox Autocephalous Church of Albania has been entirely rebuilt and enjoyed great progress. The practice of religion slowly returned. According to the "Creative Efforts" published by The Autocephalous Church of Albania, 460 parishes have been organised and catechism, preaching, and liturgical life has returned to most cities and villages. But religious observance and practice is still generally lax today. Polls have shown that, compared to the populations of other countries, few Albanians consider religion to be a dominant factor in their lives. When asked about their own religion, Albanians usually refer to the historical religious legacy of their parents or ancestors and not to their own choice of faith.

It is strange that I related this journey along "The Land of Transformation" to Mother Teresa. Mother Teresa was born on 26 August 1910 into a Kosovar Albanian family in Skopje, North Macedonia, where we were the week before. She was baptized in Skopje the day after her birth. She considered the day of her baptism, i.e. 27 August 1910, her "true birthday". Her family lived in Skopje until 1934, when they moved to Tirana. Her parents, Nikola and Dranafile Bojaxhiu were of Albanian descent.

In visiting Albania's capital Tirana, I was informed that I would be delving into the past and present of a country that had seen intense turmoil since it was founded in the 1600s. I witnessed proud monuments and brand-new projects (with some remnant of disintegrating soviet-era buildings) standing side-by-side. An equestrian statue of a national hero stands as the city's focal point, with beautiful pastel buildings surrounding Skanderbeg Square.

On the north end of the Square stands the modernist National History Museum containing exhibits covering prehistoric times through the Communist rule and the anti-Communist uprisings. Each building, monument, mural, or painting depicts its own emotionally charged story to tell, whether it is about the daily life during the time of Ottoman or during the period of oppression in the 20th-century the country rediscovered itself after decades of isolationism under communist rule. With the collapse of communism, it began to develop closer ties with other countries of Western Europe and the United States. At the time of our visit, Albania had already achieved its foreign policy ambition to integrate into the world's modern economic and security organizations. It is already a full member of NATO and was among the first Southeast European countries to join the partnership for the peace programme. It got candidate status for the EU in June 2014 in recognition of its progress in reforming its institutions to meet EU standards. However, Albania is not expected to join the EU soon, not at least until after 2020...

I have long realized that we could never understand every aspect of the lifestyle, custom and cultural life of the people we come across, not even of those within the very country and place we live. That in all aspects of our lives we must make our own choices. Every choice we make along the "way" will have consequences for the journey we take in order "to come unto the knowledge of the truth.": -1 Timothy 2:4 (KJV). "knowledge" in this text is "epignosis" in Greek, which means the coming of salvific or transformational knowing. It is not informational knowing! It is the God-centred personal spiritual knowing as we journey through this life. May we be guided and know to walk His way...

Journey to Antarctica

I saw a picture of Antarctica when I was just a little child. Later, I read the story of Amundsen. With our geography lessons at schools, most of us had already learned that Antarctica is the continent situated in the Southern Hemisphere. It is twice the size of Australia. It is noted in recorded history as the last region to be discovered. European maps continued to show this hypothetical land until Captain James Cook's ships, HMS Resolution & Adventure, came within about 120 km of the Antarctic coast before retreating in the face of an ice field in January 1773.

Antarctica has adventure in its bones. Despite the stark and inhospitable environments, legendary travellers were drawn there. Ronald Amundsen and Robert Scott famously raced to the South Pole in 1911, with Amundsen's expedition beating Scott's by 33 days. But perhaps the most famous explorer to this hostile land is Ernest Shackleton, the leader of a crew that set off in 1914. Shackleton's ship, the Endurance, was crushed in the ice in the Weddell Sea in 1916. They drifted on ice floes and eventually landed on Elephant Island, from where unbelievably, the explorer eventually delivered his entire crew to safety and civilization. Getting to Antarctica is still difficult and hazardous. Long before reaching there, sailing vessels must cross the Drake Passage, an often very tumultuous waterway, considered by some, including myself, a hallmark of high adventure in itself

Unseen until 1820, Antarctica remains a mysterious and hostile land. It is also at the same time a fragile environment. To get there also depends on how "feisty" the notorious Drake Passage is, especially if someone is prone to motion sickness. The stretch of open ocean separating Cape Horn from Paradise Bay is a nasty stretch of sea. Many stories are written or told about the hazards of sailing around the Horn. On a previous journey (as seen in these photos taken in 2011), I experienced the fury of this stretch. Our ship swayed very violently indeed. Charles Darwin wrote: "one sight of such a coast is enough to make a landsman dream for a week about shipwrecks, peril and death."

Even though Antarctica is the least-visited and least-known continent in the world, today, some cruise ships do sail close enough for their passengers to pass majestic blue icebergs. At my age, I know my own threshold of adventure. So, when I discovered that a cruise ship, "Celebrity Eclipse" would sail to Paradise Bay, I grabbed the opportunity to get onboard. Paradise Bay is a harbour in West Antarctica, one of only two cruise ships. The Argentine and Chilean scientific bases are also located here. The best time to visit Antarctica is between November and March when the sun rises above the horizon, and the sea ice melts enough to allow access. That would also be a perfect time to travel to the southern hemisphere for a "change." Change, in the right context, is a good thing. Let others say, "Nay." When we live in a country of mountains and lakes, forests and rivers, the freezing cold and seemingly desolate Southernmost continent in its "summer" make us more appreciative of the things we have at home.

On this journey, the weather was kind to us. On this particular day, Antarctica possessed an unimaginable quality. The sky was clear, and the sea blue and relatively calm. Dramatic icebergs and ice floes floated off in the distance. It was inspirational. I had the indescribable feeling of being just a small speck nearby this enormous and harsh but serenely beautiful land. I let my mind soared in a place that is almost "free of the footprints of humankind." This was magical. Since the end of the 19th century, some have longed to follow in Shackleton's footsteps to explore this polar region. Fortunately, more opportunities are now opened for us modern adventurers to check off the most elusive continent from our bucket lists. Yet few are fortunate enough even to get a glimpse of Antarctica. This changed for me. In February 2020, I found the opportunity to do so. I am one of those who can claim to have crossed the Antarctic Circle. This article may not excite real Antarctica adventurers. Nor can I shoehorn all I had experienced into this article. Few of us are the likes of Ronald Amundson and Robert Falcon Scott. I did enter "the land of the Midnight sun" to a world without the border as far south as 64°53'30.5"S – 62°57'12.8"W. I experienced a sensory overload as I had never felt before. Not since I first saw the picture of an iceberg as a little kid!

I had flown from Vancouver via Toronto to Buenos Aries with perhaps a little "flygskam" (to borrow a word from Greta Thunberg) to catch the ship bound for Paradise Bay, Antarctica. The second leg of the Air Canada flight from Toronto (with a brief stopover at Santiago) to Buenos Aires was long, but it was not particularly tedious. It had never been customary for me to pay attention to seatmates on planes. Not even on long hauls. However, there was something about this colourful girl (with a short lock of blond hair covering her forehead and a tattoo on her forearm) who drew my attention. She was sitting next to May, who was in the middle seat. This girl had removed her shoes, bent her knees, and put her feet on the back of the seat in front of her. I was tempted to counsel her on etiquette, decorum, respect, and consideration for others. But I relented and closed my eyes. At that moment, I recalled an incident of being told by a youngster, many years ago, that I was not a Canadian. This boy had said to me that "nice Canadians" never tell others what to do or not to do! I have since wondered whether that "nicety" is a virtue. Not before long, as I opened my eyes again, I noticed that the girl had already taken down her feet and settled back to her laptop. I turned towards the back of the plane to have a quick look to see how full the plane was. I noticed an Asian woman (sitting two rows behind us) wearing a face mask even though health experts and the CDC specifically do not recommend the masks for healthy people to protect themselves against COVID-19. It is no surprise that face masks are in short supply, as the simplicity of those recommendations from experts was perhaps unsettling to those who are anxious and think they can do more to protect themselves

At the time of writing this article, I realized that I had already done 43 cruises around the world, sailing the 5 Oceans (ancient people say the "7 Seas") to the seven continents. Some geographers contend that there should only be five continents. However, in the widely accepted view, there are seven continents all in all: Asia, Africa, Europe, North America, Australia, South America, and Antarctica.

But among 29 of my travel Blogs http://www.freepilgrim.com only two articles mentioned cruising. As this journey revolves mostly around cruising, the narrative should at least follow briefly on this subject. We are now on our way to Paradise Bay by Celebrity Eclipse. My feeling was that this modern ship had not been built with only the millennials in mind. The wonderful designers had realized that the older folks, with the time and money, are the ones who cruise frequently. Mobility problems come with advancing age. This was taken into consideration. I observed that it was quite easy for people to use walkers or scooters to manoeuvre to find seats, especially in the Oceanview cafe.

Unfortunately, even though they had built the ship upscale, there was not a proper library in sight. The "bookshelf" designated as "Library" was really designed and set up more for aesthetic and not for intellectual purpose. Even though I enjoyed talking to other passengers, especially if they choose to sit at the table next to us in the Oceanview Café, I could not interact all day without being exhausted. I would often walk up the stairs to the 15th deck to read the books that I had downloaded with the Kindle App until my eyes needed to take in the serenity of the open sea.

The Oceanview buffet had a decent variety and labelled according to the various diet issues, e.g., glutton free, sugar-free, dairy, etc. The waiters were helpful and eager to replace anything we wanted to try. However, I thought the stocked colourful mass-produced desserts (including the variety of captivating doughnuts) of mix sour and sweet look merely tantalizing and appealing but were seldom satisfying to the sophisticated palates. And by His grace, there was an abundance! But when it comes to food, I am often reminded of the story of Elijah and the widow of Zarepath: - 1 King 17:10-15. Perhaps prophet Elijah was a man who understood the concept that less is more

We have now left Paradise Bay, passed Elephant Island and on our way to the Falkland Islands. A thunders storm of considerable severity had rumbled continuously through the night. We could hear it while resting in the comfort of our cabin. Nevertheless, we had the advantage of a glorious morning with cool Antarctic fresh air. As I looked yonder, I saw large white clouds sailing above the deep blue sea. I could imagine and enter fully into the feeling of a certain sailor, who, while approaching Stanley, Falkland rubbed his hands in glee and exclaimed, "Now, this is what I like!" A lovely country it is ...with an old-fashioned world look about it. It appears to have resisted the so-called modern improvements. It is original beauty not suffered. It has a mellow, peaceful, and restful look about it with some comfortable looking timbered houses and gardens filled with old-fashioned flowers. The Islands are home mostly to sheep farms and fisheries. It is also in that part of the mild Antarctic zone "bio-geographically" connected to flora and fauna of Patagonia in mainland South America. The capital Stanley sits on East Falkland, which is the largest island. The Christ Church Cathedral, consecrated in 1892, is the southernmost Anglican cathedral in the world.

The United Kingdom and Argentina both claimed the Falkland Islands resulting in a 10-week undeclared war between Argentina and the United Kingdom in 1982. The conflict began on 2 April, when Argentina invaded and occupied the Falkland Islands, followed by the invasion of South Georgia the next day. The British government dispatched a naval task force on 5 April to engage the Argentine Navy and Air Force before making an amphibious assault on the islands.

The conflict lasted 74 days and ended with an Argentine surrender on 14 June, returning the islands to British control. In the middle of this conflict, I remember talking about this with my golfing partner Graham Steel at the Sabah Golf and Country club. In 2009 The British prime minister (Gordon Brown) had a meeting with the Argentine president (Cristina Fernández de Kirchner) and said that there would be no further talks over the sovereignty of the Falklands. The UK bases its position on its continuous administration of the islands since 1833 and the islanders' "right to self-determination as set out in the UN Charter". In March 2013, the Falkland Islands held a referendum on its political status: 99.8% of votes cast favoured remaining a British overseas territory.

Is it true that "in talking about the past we lie with every breath we draw", as William Maxwell once stated? Or are we merely misinterpreting the past? I am also not suggesting that some anthropologists, archaeologists, historians, and others attempt to spin and twist the realities of the past. I only think that we cannot hope to feel or to comprehend what the past was really like if we see it through the lens of this era and through our modern (and too often Western) eyes. Indeed, bringing up the past (as we see it) in our time is intrinsically and fundamentally the problem. The people of times gone by did not simply 'view' events. They lived it!

As I walked around this memorial, I could not help feeling sad for those affected by this senseless conflict. I pictured the soldiers as some whose lives confirmed that "the good died young." We always quote a variation of the adage that those who fail to remember the past are condemned to repeat it. People who lived through an event such as this become the authoritative bearers, not merely of a tale to be told (of what it was really like), but more importantly, a lesson to be learned. The memory of an event like this can act as a witness with a kind of moral force. This moral witness can offer to ensure some measure of justice: if it is not "never again," then at least "lest we forget."

We stayed for a while around this memorial, trying to understand the significance of it all. Perhaps all human conflicts are the result of man's sin – false pride: - www.freepilgrim.com/the-road-to-corinth/. I then went and sat on the low stone wall nearby and tasted the joy of my own inner peace. After a good rest here and a stroll along the sea wall, we ventured further to explore the old-fashioned beauty of this island. We passed many wayside cottages with very well-maintained gardens, all showing love for flowers. The cottages have an old-world look about them with no attempt at building design or beauty. Yet, they were natural and picturesque. Those cottages were irregular and unique in contrast to the uniformed constructions of the modern ones. Did the builders think of outside appearance? Perhaps not. Perhaps they just planned the rooms, passages, the interior, windows, and chimneys where they were most required and needed. Those lovely cottages suggested to me, as a passer-by, that comfort inside is achieved without seeking it. They appeared so well built that they had not needed nor received many restorations or repairs.

From what we saw as we passed by, we concluded and had the impression that the town and buildings would be much the same a century hence. We wanted to see more, but dark, ominous clouds were gathering around in all directions. The distant rumblings warned us that rain and possibly a thunderstorm might be approaching. We passed the "Penguin News" and save for a few drops of rain and the continuous distant rumblings, we, in some strange manner, escaped the thunderstorm which other passengers experienced. As we strolled through the village, a few cars passed by, but the place appeared to be in a peaceful sleep. We left it sleeping – and no doubt it will still be asleep should we ever pass this way again.

So, we say "Goodbye"! Soon we will be heading back to Buenos Aries to catch the Island Princess for the merrymaking and festivity of the carnival atmosphere in Rio de Janeiro before Shrove Tuesday and then onwards in Lent to the Devil's Island... But that is another story...

A Continuing Journey
Of Belief And Faith

You could say I am a cradle-Christian. I grew up in a household that went to church on Sunday and in which Christianity was practised. Does being a cradle-Christian make me more as a follower of Christ? "the cradle-Christian may be unable to discern the influence of the Holy Spirit in his life": -IIItyd Trethowan. I had just thought about belief and faith (and the difference between them). When my father told me that he would be taking us to picnic at Batu Sapi, I believed him. I knew he would take us there. I had faith in him.

Belief -

But I have only been a cultural Christian. How do we view other Christians? There is a third person in each one of us. This third person is what Thomas Merton called our "true self". Who we are in our fullness is known only to God. Therefore, our truest identity requires seeking and discovering God. Each one's relationship with God is unique. No one can set a path, way, or method for someone else to follow because that would mean diverging the other's spiritual journey. Only God can lead us by the Holy Spirit, and it is up to each believer to discover and respond to the Holy Spirit. But first, we must believe in the Holy Spirit.

Whether we believe this is as true and timeless as the human quest for authenticity. More importantly, if we do not believe, the quest for authenticity will lead us nowhere. But belief is the product of what we think. It is a product of our mind. Because we live in a fallen world, our mind is already disadvantaged, and we constantly run in trouble. Most likely, our belief is rooted in our upbringing and culture and, to a certain extent in our education. Our belief can be in direct conflict with what we know is true. Sometimes belief shifts because of peer pressures. We change our attitudes, values, or behaviours to conform to those who influence us. Belief can change with cultural norm!

Faith -

Faith is an attitude of accepting that we do not know. It is different from belief. If we know then faith is unnecessary. Knowing does not create faith. We remain humble to not know in the context of faith. "Humble yourselves in the sight of the Lord, and he shall lift you up.": -James4:10.

St. Benedict also emphasized humility to overcome self-will. Self-will is that inherent tendency within us to get our own way. It manifests a deep self-centeredness that is debilitating because it gets in the way of loving God and our neighbour- which is the only way for us to find joy and fulfillment. Unlike belief, the Christian faith is the product of the Holy Spirit. Faith is a living, bold trust in grace. Faith is God's grace working in us. This grace kills the old Adam and makes us completely different people. It transforms us and gives new birth. "which were born, not of blood, nor of the will of the flesh, nor of the will of man, but of God": -John 1:13.

Wisdom -

This blog is written amid the Coronavirus (covid-19) pandemic. We are all fearful. Fear and faith have something in common. They both ask us to believe in something we cannot see. Fear is the absence of faith or that faith that does not work. Fear fills the cracks in our mind and our heart in the absence of faith. Faith is the certainty that we get the support we need to overcome this crisis. Wisdom is the ability to take the support and turn it into the resources we need. Should we rely purely on faith in this crisis? The answer is Prayer, prevention, and protection and in that order. It is important to be prepared. God gives us the wisdom to discern what is required of us.

BUENOS AIRES

In the middle of the Coronavirus outbreak, we arrived Buena Aires by air from Toronto as related in my blog:- http://www.freepilgrim.com/journey-to-antarctica/. As we had watched the movie "The Two Popes", we decided to visit the Metropolitan Cathedral of Buenos Aires where Pope Francis once served as Archbishop. The story in the movie written by Anthony McCarten contain narratives that visualize scenes behind the walls of the Vatican where conservative Pope Benedict XVI and liberal Pope Francis had to find common grounds to forge a new path for the Catholic Church. The Metropolitan Cathedral of Buenos Aires is the main Catholic church located in the city centre, overlooking Plaza de Mayo, in the San Nicolás neighbourhood. This was where Archbishop Jorge Bergoglio (now Pope Francis) used to perform mass before assuming office in the Vatican in 2013.

Cathedral & Revelation -

The Metropolitan Cathedral of Buenos Aires also houses a museum that exhibits some of Pope Francis's personal and liturgical objects. As a pilgrim, I have the tendency to visit churches whenever I visit a new place and find myself as a stranger in town. Although I love to see old churches with their colourful paintings, artefacts, and mosaics, I am no longer visiting them merely for the arts. Today there is something more that attracts me: a kind of interior peace. I sat down on the side of the pew at the back of this Cathedral. The place was quite full for a Sunday on February 2nd, 2020. The people consisted of young, middle-aged, and old. There was something that distinguished them from the congregation in the Anglican Church of Canada that I have come across. They also sat in silence. I liked that. I love the silence despite the size of the congregation. I found peace in it. I ceased to view the worshippers with criticism. It is Christ who established His Church, among other reasons that we may seek salvation. The Holy Spirit draws us to Christ through the action and encouragement of our fellow men.

What a revelation it was to discover many ordinary people in a place together, more conscious of God than of one another, showing off their ornaments or clothes or the way they dressed. They were there probably purely to fulfil a Christian obligation. In some churches I know, we were there to have one eye or the corner of an eye for a member or congregation member. Sometimes with the whole of both of our eyes. The altar with something or other I could not see very well, but the people were praying by themselves, and I have absorbed in the thing as a whole: the business of the altar and the people. Seeing the late comers hastily genuflecting before entering the pew, I realised my omission. I got the idea that at least one person had spotted me for a pagan and waiting for me to miss a few more genuflects before giving me a reproof. Soon we all stood up. I did not know or understand what the purpose of it was. I eventually figured out that the priest was going to read the gospel—the Good News in this troubled time in our fallen worlds.

It is now past Ash Wednesday. By now, we had already been informed of the problem with Diamond Princess. The vessel's passengers were to be tested for coronavirus at the Terminal in Yokohama, south of Tokyo. Meanwhile, we were on the Island Princess, and our journey continued to Devil's Island. I had a glimpse of the place where tens of thousands of prisoners were doomed to live lives of servitudes on what came to be known as the colony of the dammed. We attended a non-denominational Sunday Service on board and all hymns were familiar to us, which I enjoyed singing and praising Him. At that moment, I was thinking that St. Augustine must have touched something special and smooth because he was thinking about singing and praying to God. Perhaps that was why he said: "to sing is to pray twice."

TRINIDAD & FOREFATHERS

Our ship called Trinidad, an island my great grandfather and his family stayed (for a while) on their way back to China from British Guiana, where they had worked as indentured labourers in the late 1800s. There, we met a taxi driver of the Khan clan from India, not from Pakistan. His forefathers arrived in Trinidad and Tobago around the time my forefathers were there. I told him I had a close Muslim acquaintance in Sabah by the name of Majid Khan whose brother Khayyam (a carpet dealer) used to sell us beautiful rugs for my house on Signal Hill. As he was taking us to Saint Benedict Abbey, he pre-emptively told us that he is not Muslim but a converted Christian of the Pentecostal denomination in Trinidad, who believed that revisionist theology on gay marriage violates God's intentional design. His conversion to Christianity also appeared to me that Dakwah, central to contemporary Islamic thought, was conspicuously absent in Trinidad.

Benedictine Monastery

The Saint Benedictine Abbey, established in 1912, situated high up on a hill 1300 metres above sea level, is an active Benedictine monastery following the Order of St. Benedict. This monastery is located in the northwestern town of St. Augustine in Tunapuna–Piarco in Trinidad and Tobago. The Benedictine Order was founded by Saint Benedict of Nuria, who wrote The Rule of Saint Benedict, followed by all Benedictines. The Abbey reminded us of our visit to Sacro Speco in Subiaco, Italy, where we spent considerable time. Ref: http://www.freepilgrim.com/solitude/ Benedict, born in 480 in Nursia, Italy, was sent by his family to Rome to study law. Revolted by the immorality of the city, he decided to spend his days in seclusion and prayer. Young Benedict gained a following and established the Benedictine order. The motto of the Benedictine Order is "Ora et Labora" - 'Pray and Work'.

Today, with its tower and red roofs, Saint Benedict Abbey consists of a church, a monastery, a seminary, a drug rehabilitation centre, and a yogurt factory. It welcomes and draws people of all faiths seeking solace, peace, and fulfilment. Beside the spiritual purpose, we also enjoyed the view from the hillside which offered a pristine lookout over the surrounding forests and the town below.

Gone by 2040?

On our way back to the ship from the taxi stand where Khan dropped us off, we came across (as if by accident) The Holy Trinity Cathedral of Trinidad and Tobago. This Cathedral is an Anglican cathedral located in the heart of the capital, Port of Spain. It was built in the 1800s. Its architecture is of that period with beautiful stain-glass windows in a mosaic of colours. As I was sitting on one of the back pews inside, in silence, I was reminded of a paper I wrote in early 2008 entitled "The end of Anglicanism in Canada?". Before we left on this journey, I read an article in the Anglican Journal that confirmed what I had believed way back in early 2000. I feel very sad for the Anglican Church of Canada.

Gifts & extended adolescence

At Barbados, we were led, I believe (with perfect timing) by the Holy Spirit to the St. Mary's church to witness a children choir practising. These adorable children appeared to be more "with it" and "in it" than we were as we listened to their gifted voice...I knew they were not just singing but singing from their hearts. In a strange way, they minded me of an incident at which I was told not to sing.

Most of my friends and relatives know I was a child chorister at our church in Sandakan. One evening in Advent, a long time ago, when I was around 12 or 13 years old, we went out to sing carols at the home of the General Manager of Harrisons & Crossfield. Both my father and our Choir Master were the staff of this British trading company. The boss was entertaining guests at Company's Christmas party. In the middle of our singing, my Choir Master quietly signalled me to stop singing. I was naturally hurt. It turned out that my voice was breaking as I was in transition from a child to a young adult (and eventually to manhood). I am thankful to have lived in that era when boys became men. It is observed that too many boys and young men today are stuck in the stage of extended adolescence. Young men are now spending most of their time on video games, Netflix, internet trolling. In this new "pre-adulthood", many are avoiding adult responsibilities- including marriage. We are now living in a new age in a society that has a lot of confusion about what men are good for. Men are often over criticized as being misogynistic and/or aggressive. Some psychologists have argued that the rise of women has turned men into boys. Being raised in the eastern culture and educated in conservative England in the early sixties, I like to think they are right. But I really do not know. Others have said it is rubbish to think so. Who am I to say they are wrong, and those psychologists are right.

NELSON DRUNKEN SAILOR & ST. JOHN

Since 2012 it has been my intention to revisit Antigua from where a couple of our friends in our parish of St. John's have originated. May and I visited this island eight years ago. The famous British Vice-Admiral Horatio Nelson (who was created 1st Viscount Nelson in 1801) of the Napoleonic wars was Senior Naval Officer of the Leeward Islands and stationed on Antigua. We had on the previous occasion visited the famous Nelson Dockyard where a story of a sailor by the name of William Clarke had been told. "Think of me tonight with a woman in my arms and a bottle of rum in my belly," said William Clarke to his fellow seamen in Antigua's English Harbour. On one other occasion, this sailor was found guilty by court-martial for his behaviour. Nelson, as commanding officer of the frigate Boreas, spared him from hanging.

But the real reason I wanted to revisit the island was to have the opportunity to see the process of restoration of the Anglican cathedral of our parish namesake. The restoration of this old building is a costly and technically challenging endeavour that is rife with uncertainty.

Third (3rd) Incarnation

This Cathedral is now in its 3rd "incarnation". The earthquakes in 1683 and in 1745 destroyed the structures, and the Cathedral has also "suffered" Category 4 hurricane and the cruelty of time. "Time neither respects persons nor things. None–not even imposing buildings and monuments–can withstand the passage of time unscathed without at least some help." There is a donation box near the Font for those who do not want the left hand to know what the right-hand does. Many have helped in this 3rd "incarnation". I hope my friends from Antigua will see services in this historical pillar of this country's Christian identity one day.

It was now passed First Sunday in Lent, and we were cruising back to Fort Lauderdale from where we would take our flight home. But the Coronavirus (covid-19) epidemic was beginning to create uncertainty. Many cruise ships had been turned away from Caribbean ports or had to anchor offshore under quarantine. For weeks, New Yorkers braced for the arrival of the coronavirus. Governor Andrew M. Cuomo, on first Sunday in Lent (March 1st, 2020) confirmed New York State's first case of the coronavirus, saying that a woman contracted the virus while travelling in Iran and was now in New York City isolated in her home. CDC had already warned of a pandemic. Even if we were allowed to disembark, we would still have to fly to LaGuardia Airport in New York. There is no direct flight from Fort Lauderdale to Vancouver. The transit time at busy LaGuardia is 4 hours. Where would we be tonight? I was reminded of the time we were on the Camino, not knowing (after the first week) where we would be spending the nights. But at the end of the day, and in all the following evenings thereafter, God showed us a la casa. So, by His grace, we got home safe and healthy and slept in our own bed!

We are living in a fallen world. It is hard to hold on to our faith in these troubled times. I will try to understand and take a lesson from the Book of Job. Job was a good man, and yet God allowed Satan to do what he did. Though God called Job blameless and upright, when God showed Job his sin, he repented: not just superficially but with deep, sincere remorse and sorrow. I have faith in God. I am confident that in the end, God will see us through this crisis.

About the Author

Born in 1942 in British North Borneo (Sabah Malaysia), and now residing in Vancouver, British Columbia, Canada, Nicholas Fung trained as a Barrister-at-Law at The Honourable Society of The Inner Temple and was called to the Bar of England and Wales in 1966. Eventually returned to Sabah; he initiated the formation and was the First Secretary of the Sabah Law Association. He served as the State Attorney-General and was founder and president of The Council of The Justices of The Peace and a founding member of The Sabah Golf and Country Club. Appointed by the Central Bank of Malaysia, he was tasked with restructuring the bank (which has merged with Alliance Bank Malaysia). It is from this position that he ultimately retired.

That is when his journey truly began. Searching for a spiritual path, he started making pilgrimages around the world while discovering himself- an undertaking with no clear destination but of inestimable value. Nicholas cherishes engaging with people worldwide to hear stories from diverse cultures and hoping to counter bigotry with knowledge and encourage others to see that peace can be achieved even when there are differences between us. With that dedication, he hopes to inspire others--to open a space in their busy secular lives and allow for deep and profound personal transformation.

In *Free Pilgrim* and *Free Pilgrim 2*, Nicholas Fung took his readers on a physical, spiritual, and mystical path around the world, visiting countless and inspirational sites, both modern and ancient. The books are available online and from https://books.friesenpress.com/store. The author may be reached at: nncfung2@gmail.com

In *Free Pilgrim 3*, the Author returns to his place of birth, "The Land Below The Wind". Even though he had made similar trips back before, he yet strangely discovered that he still arrived "where he had started and knew the place for the first time." His insightful writing clearly illustrates both the divine and mundane nature of humanity. We are all one people, though separated by great distances, continents, and millenniums, that humanity shines through in our great works, beauties, and cultures of the world around us

With another ten adventures, *Free Pilgrim 3* will awaken your drive to discover new places, learn about a new culture and perhaps have a little more understanding of who we are as a human collective. While there is nothing more informative and transformative than taking a physical pilgrimage to incredible places, these books are as close as one can get without leaving the armchairs and setting out on our own. But if you are fortunate enough, incline and have the time, these narratives may inspire you to do just that.

CPSIA information can be obtained
at www.ICGtesting.com
Printed in the USA
BVHW021521061021
618020BV00010B/22